ABANDONED BY FAMILY
BUT NEVER BY
GOD

A Personal Journey Through Neglect, Abuse, Mental Illness and Recovery

B. A. Marks

ISBN 978-1-63630-393-2 (Paperback)
ISBN 978-1-63630-394-9 (Digital)

Copyright © 2020 B. A. Marks
All rights reserved
First Edition

Cover Artwork by Maya

All rights reserved. No part of this publication may be reproduced, distributed, or transmitted in any form or by any means, including photocopying, recording, or other electronic or mechanical methods without the prior written permission of the publisher. For permission requests, solicit the publisher via the address below.

Covenant Books, Inc.
11661 Hwy 707
Murrells Inlet, SC 29576
www.covenantbooks.com

To all the children and adults suffering:
Let go and give your burdens to the Lord.
There is a freedom in doing this!
Life is what you make it. You are not your circumstances!
Your past does not determine your future, your choices do!

ACKNOWLEDGMENTS

God my Father and my Savior Jesus Christ. I thank you for putting my feelings and experiences into words, and for never leaving me!

My daughters: I appreciate you both, and I love you to infinity. Thank you for accepting my quirks and shortcomings. My life would be empty without you. Equally, you both fill my heart with joy and hope.

My dear friends: I thank you all for the support and encouraging words you have always given me. You have helped immensely and have kept me motivated while writing this book. A special thanks to Yousif. I appreciate you teaching me how to laugh again. I could not have done as much growing had it not been for your unwavering friendship.

Boz! You are an amazing man. I admire you a great deal! Thank you for all of your invaluable advice and encouragement. Without you, my friend, I would have remained in a deep depression for much longer than I did. You taught me how to love myself and believe, in what I thought, was the right path for me to pursue. I love your heart, and your deeply apparent faith, in my abilities to better myself. I thank you!

Thank you to my Healing Team at Easter Seals of Michigan, Centerline, Michigan. I have learned something from each person I have had the pleasure to work with. My therapists stretched my mind and thinking, making me realize I no longer had to be my worst critic. My caseworkers helped me find housing, never giving up on me. They gave me so many resources. Without my nurse practitioner, my medications would not have been a perfect match for me. Thanks for showing me I am still relevant to society!

CONTENTS

Foreword 9

Chapter 1 11
Chapter 2 16
Chapter 3 21
Chapter 4 28
Chapter 5 32
Chapter 6 37
Chapter 7 42
Chapter 8 48
Chapter 9 54
Chapter 10 58
Chapter 11 62
Chapter 12 66
Chapter 13 74
Chapter 14 80
Chapter 15 85
Chapter 16 93
Chapter 17 99
Chapter 18 105
Chapter 19 112
Chapter 20 118
Chapter 21 123
Chapter 22 128
Chapter 23 133
Chapter 24 141
Chapter 25 147
Chapter 26 152

Chapter 27 158
Chapter 28 165
Chapter 29 170
Chapter 30 179
Chapter 31 187

Resources 193

FOREWORD

I have been asked to write this foreword for Barb's new work concerning her journey through life. Being asked by this special woman is both an honor and privilege. I have known Barb for over a decade, and our relationship working together has been an enriching experience for me. I have gained an important "insider's view" of an extraordinary woman.

We hold and gaze at a diamond in all its magnificence, but do we ever stop to reflect on its journey? The diamond is a product of constant and extreme forces of nature. Those forces cause a metamorphosis to take place, and then a piece of coal becomes something priceless and unique. We become a witness to something breathtaking and a product of those previous vicissitudes throughout its history. Yet, when we look upon the final product, it does not give testimony to its previous journey of transformation.

This book takes us into the journey and history of an individual diamond named Barb. She has withstood, persevered, and overcome great subjective personal trials and pressures. These circumstances brought unforeseen development into making Barb who she is today! This is a personal journey through a hellish, painful, and extraordinarily complex, always difficult life. Yet her testimony found within these pages will allow you to be privy to her transformation and transmutation of existence, into a life now rich and fully productive!

Barb's story, her journey, her sweat and tears can be felt and touched in the pages of this book. Prepare to be entertained and have your breath taken away. This read is about a lifelong struggle, against great odds, and a championing onward to have become someone who truly is a priceless treasure. To know and behold the makings of a diamond from stone into a polished final product.

Dr. Philip Greenberg

> Happy is anyone who shows consideration to the lowly
> one. God will rescue him in the day of calamity.
> —Psalms 41:1

CHAPTER 1

My earliest memories of my *born-into family* developed in the summer of 1970. I, months away from my fourth birthday, had an in-home babysitter. I remember Millicent well; she watched both my brother Danny and myself. Millicent was a huge woman who sat on the south end of the couch, never moving. She was dirty-looking, uncouth, and did not participate in playing with us. I do not recall ever eating lunch; and Danny and I fended for ourselves that summer. Millicent did not know where we were most of the time, so Danny and I escaped out of the boy's bedroom window one afternoon. We played outside for hours, until my mom came home from work. When she pulled into the driveway, we were standing on the front lawn, and she was visibly upset. We explained to her what happened while she was at work, and why we climbed out of the window. Millicent was asleep when my mom walked in the door. She was fired instantly.

In late summer of 1971, I was told by my mom that I would be staying with a family who had a teenaged daughter. I was assured I would be returning home, but never knew when. I recall arriving at the Kay's in August. I was kept in the dark about why I was not living at home with my born-into family.

Soon afterward, I realized I spent more time with Kate and Ian Kay than with my mom or siblings. My mom said, years later, she came to get me every weekend. That, I have no recollection of. I do remember getting on a bike and attempting to ride back to my mom. I became afraid even though I knew how to get there. I turned back around, approximately one and a half miles from the Kay's; I was almost five years old.

I began attending kindergarten two blocks from Aunt Kate's home, in September of that year. I was officially living with the Kay's and their daughter Mona full-time. Their house was on 8 Mile and Kelly across from Eastland Mall. Ours was at Outer Drive and Mound Road. It was a good eight to ten miles away from one other. They were "Aunt Kate" and "Uncle Ian" to me, realizing they really were not. I cannot recall at what moment I found out my mom contacted Kate Kay from an ad in the church paper, just like Millicent. However, living with the Kay's would prove to be consequentially beneficial to me in the long term.

Aunt Kate also took care of another little girl, and perhaps her brother at times. Dana was my playmate. We rode bikes together, had tea parties, and played beneath the saucer magnolia tree in the backyard. We had fun running through the sprinkler and learning how to make our own peanut butter and jelly sandwiches. I remember her well. I was turning five years old, Dana was four.

I do not remember caring about my born-into family much. After all, I really did not know them. I now occupied my time learning and being loved by the Kay's. They taught me common sense thinking, and how a regular family functioned. Mona was much older than I. She attended Marygrove College on Detroit's west side. Mona was studious, hip, and studied ballet. I had the opportunity to hang out with her and her friends, and that was always a treat for me. Mona, on occasion, took me to the college, and I watched her perform the art of ballet. I learned a lot from observing her.

I began to listen to music she liked and immediately felt the groove of the rhythm. The album *Peace Train* by Cat Stevens played all the time. Mona liked him a lot, and I liked what she liked. Cat Stevens spoke to me in ways the adults did not. He gave me the benefit of the doubt. *Moonshadow, Oh Very Young,* and *Can't Keep It In* were my favorite hits. Mona clearly understood why I was there, even though I had no clue. I knew my dad was ill in the brain, and my mom worked hard for Chrysler, providing for her six children. At least five of them, I thought. I was the last born, in a house full of five additional children, ranging in ages from six to fifteen. My mother, for whatever reason, could not give proper attention to me. That was the extent of my knowledge. I did, however, get attention from Mona, and it was the kind a big sister would give.

At Aunt Kate's home, among other things, I was taught how to tie my shoes. I remember my mom coming to pick me up one weekend, and I excitedly showed her what I had learned. I sat upon Uncle Ian's lap as I tied my very own laces. I would retain a memorable moment at that young age. *Why didn't my mom teach me this?* Similar questions filled my mind, but I rationalized them all away by reminding myself Aunt Kate and Uncle Ian were my extended family. That meant love, respect, and lessons. I received all of those.

In my early childhood, I recall making coffee for Uncle Ian and Aunt Kate. I prepared it with cream and sugar, delivering it to their respective coffee tables. I learned to make a bed, military style, clean, cook, and garden. I was taught to be a tidy girl. I played constructively and used my imagination freely. I learned by watching *Sesame Street, The Electric Company, Captain Kangaroo,* and of course, *Kimba. The Electric Company* was my favorite: "Conjunction junction, what's your function, hooking up words and phrases and clauses."

Aunt Kate and Mona were master seamstresses. I watched intently as they crafted blouses, vests, and pants. I played in the *button box* during that time, usually sitting on the floor, beside the sewing machine. Always keeping an eye on what their steps were, I repeatedly asked questions about what they were doing, and they attentively answered.

In the summer of 1972, I became a quick study on independence. I was in Port Austin, Michigan, with the Kay's. I was listening to Simon and Garfunkel's "Cecilia" and "Mrs. Robinson." Mona introduced me to great music, which was expressing love and kindness, melodies I fell in love with. I played in the gardens and on the outskirts of the woods while on the Kay's property. I frequented Clark's Penny Candy Store, and the library, both of which were in town. My job was to clean and play, and that was what I did. Everyone in town seemingly knew who I was; I felt very protected.

Uncle Ian had a riding lawnmower. I loved the smell of gasoline and fresh cut grass. Uncle Ian would sit me atop his lap; as always taking me for rides around the yard while he mowed. I truly looked forward to that time with him. Most of my time was spent with Aunt Kate. It was my opportunity to be with a man. Uncle Ian did things differently because he was strong and in control. That appealed to me. He taught me about lawn care and outdoor maintenance, and I carried that information within me.

At their home up north, Uncle Ian always sat on the front, screened-in porch. He read the paper or talked with the neighbors who dropped by.

All the gentlemen, once together, conversed well into the night. I sat with them, watching the traffic of cars and the people as they walked down busy Spring Street. I was always around the men, sitting on one of the many chairs, listening intently. I gazed out of the many windows surrounding the porch. Uncle Ian loved the Detroit Tigers. I often sat upon his lap, cuddling as we listened to the games on the radio.

In the cottage, under the steps, there was a closet leading to the upstairs bedrooms. Aunt Kate had four dolls stored in there, each standing three feet high. I would prop them up on the beds that were tightly made with chenille bedspreads. I looked forward to the treat of playing with these full-sized babies because they were my height. Never able to change their clothes or comb their hair, I just played with them. Those dolls served as friends to me at the time. I recall Dana being up north, but not frequently enough. I was surrounded by adults and their conversations, but longed to play with someone my age.

That summer, Aunt Kate taught me about the general concept of gardening and flower bed design. The time spent with her was so precious to me, it seems as though it were last week. How can memories be so vivid after more than forty-five years? She was always in the sun baking her already very tanned skin. I gathered my own sense of gardening before long, and developed an interest in plants, especially perennials. I also learned about garage sales, selling flowers you grew on your land, and how to put those plants into mobile containers. Aunt Kate sold her flowering allium bulbs in a variety of colors to passersby, digging them right out of the ground. I recall thinking that was so ingenious.

Many times, as we drove to the cabin in Port Austin, Uncle Ian pulled over. Aunt Kate would pick wild flowers from the expressway edge and take them home. You would not dare do that today. She then either planted or multiplied the perennials. I watched her so intently, and I learned. I observed Aunt Kate prepare meals, constantly being on the move. She was a great teacher looking back. I never knew, at that age, what I was experiencing. I suppose a five-year-old would not be inclined to knowing.

Mona taught me in a different way. She expressed the importance of school, and in achieving your own personal goals. I would never receive that in the born-into family's house. She explained the lyrics to the popular songs of the summer to me. We listened to them together, and sometimes with her long-time friends. The best memory of Mona, though, was her Archie and the Gang comic books she received in the mail. Even before she finished reading them and wearing them out, I was always given the opportunity to glance at the pictures, reading the stories in my capacity.

Mona was a very cool young adult who always made time for me. She treated me with respect and taught me at the same time. She made it her duty to have fun with me. I knew I loved her like a big sister. It was easy to feel because of how Mona treated me. What more could I have wanted? I enjoyed being at Uncle Ian and Aunt Kate's, but I longed for my family as summer grew to an end. I could not fathom why I was not with them. I did have fun at the cottage though, learning many things. I enjoyed exploring the cemetery that sat kitty corner from the Kay's property. There was a park across the street, behind St. Mary's Convent. If I was not mingling with the locals in town, you could find me there, running alongside the merry-go-round.

The church park, as I matured, proved to be a quiet spot for me and my thoughts. I gravitated to the weeping willow tree that stood tall between the convent wall and the playground. Never having seen that kind of tree in Detroit before, it spoke to me, silently. I loved how when the wind blew, the tree then danced for me. I have ever since been drawn to them.

> You must love God with all your heart and all
> your soul and all your strength.
>
> —Deuteronomy 6:5

CHAPTER 2

I began attending St. Louis the King Catholic School in September of 1972. That remained my school for eight years. Although I have no recollection of returning home to my born into family, I clearly remember my mom taking me to Sears, at Macomb Mall, for clothes shopping. I would wear a uniform to school; however, I needed everyday clothes, including a dress with a slip. Then she and I took a trip to Junior Boot Shop, buying tennis shoes and dress shoes. I was a prepared little girl; I can remember that moment. It was uncomfortable receiving from a stranger, but somehow acceptable to me inside my mind.

Growing up in the city of Detroit during the '70s was memorable to me. I was a good girl, doing what was expected of me, and I always listened to adults in authority. I was taught that, in and out of school. My mom, the nuns, and our monsignor were very particular when it came to manners. Listening to authority and always orchestrating that, through the use of manners, were one in the same to me. Life seemed to be going smoothly, although much was expected of me. Aunt Kate had taught me how to basically take care of a home. Now that I was here, I realized how much I learned in one year's time.

Slowly, I became acclimated with my family while I attended first grade. The dynamics of the siblings were that of bickering and constant arguing. I quickly picked up on many issues my siblings had, and being angry was one. My brothers, in comparison to my sisters, had their separate problems with anger. They all had different personalities and handled matters in their own ways. I was a stranger in the home, and I noticed things a little girl may not be privy to paying attention to.

My oldest brother Jonathon (John) and I had the quickest bond. He had a soft temperament with me. His girlfriend, Lynn, was tiny and petite. Lynn and I were very kind and compassionate toward each other. We became quick buddies, similar to Mona. Lynn and John were grade school sweethearts, now in high school, and they seemed to have a great relationship because they were always together.

In first grade, while getting ready for school, my two sisters, Josephine (Josie) and Leslie, would repeatedly treat me badly. In the mornings, while preparing for my day and eating breakfast, Josie often pushed and shoved me, telling me to "Get out of the way." She took naked pictures of me while I dressed, and then she showed them to her friends, laughing and making fun of me. *Why was I here?* I thought. They did not seem to like me at all. In my young mind, I thought perhaps I had stolen my mom's attention away from them.

Josie took French at Osborn High School. She walked around saying, *"Fermer la bouche s'il vous plait,"* over and over. Translated, it meant "Shut your mouth, please." Josie did many odd things for attention. She even went so far as to change her vernacular, talking with a Boston drawl. Till this day, she still carries that accent. Even though they treated me badly, I grew to accept their behaviors and loved them anyway.

I began listening to the adult's converse. After all, that is all I had at the Kays. I heard my mom say my dad was not going to be home again. My mom told me my dad was ill, and I quickly learned the term "paranoid schizophrenia." That meant nothing to my young mind, other than the fact that I did not and would not have a daddy. I was a sad girl for many reasons, but that was harsh! I dreamt of my daddy all the time. *If I didn't have a dad, who would be there for me?* I thought.

My oldest sister Josie and I became cordial to one another over the next few months. She seemed very intelligent, always using unrecognizably big words. I knew it was her way of getting attention and showing off. We visited her boyfriends, riding the bus together. Josie, at sixteen, had many boyfriends, keeping them secrets from one another. One day I informed her of a phone call she had gotten from Richey. She literally beat me afterward for having said it in front of Ronnie. I, till this day, remember how I felt. I did not understand what I had done wrong. Of course, now I do. Mona never treated me like that and never raised her hand to me.

Josie took me to quite a few places with her. We went to Downtown Detroit frequently. The very first time I set foot in the Fisher Building was with her. Josie introduced me to the Detroit Institute of Arts also. There I fell in love with John Singer Sargent and Van Gogh. The DIA would become one of my favorite places to visit as an adult. I had an idea, in my small mind, Josie had me around to meet men. That became a truth. Even though that was happening, I absorbed every bit of the culture and took in all of the architecture of downtown.

My sisters and I shared a 10x12 bedroom. We, like the boys, had trundle beds. They were bunk beds with a third mattress on the bottom. Because I was the smallest, my mom gave me the upper bunk. Leslie always gave me a hard time when we were in the bedroom together. She and Josie both considered it "their space." I always felt as if they were just waiting for me to go away again. I never felt it was my home until high school came. My mind and soul always felt like I belonged somewhere else.

The things that belonged to Josie and Leslie were theirs. They never shared; and they continuously harassed me. There were times I got my hair fixed by one of them. Both were rough with my head, pulling and tugging on me. I learned, very quickly, how to do my own hair. Just when I thought I had it right, my mom changed my style to a shag. It was a hideous haircut, and I told my mom I did not like it at all. She told me it was the style, and that was my cut for five years. It seemed they simply did not want the added responsibility of caring for me. I was never listened to, and they thought, because Aunt Kate taught me to clean, I was their personal housekeeper.

Josie had a dresser with a set of three small drawers. She called them her "daisy drawers." I could not even look at them without getting a *glare* from the owner. *"Keep out,"* she screamed. I always listened to her, but silently wondered what was so private in there. Leslie would repeatedly loosen the upper slats of the bunk bed, so when I lay down, I would fall through to the middle bed. I was scared a lot of the time, but learned to keep my mouth shut. They always played "practical jokes" on me. I never looked at it that way. I felt it was cruel. They constantly gave me a difficult time. I missed Uncle Ian, Aunt Kate, and Mona profusely.

Once the three of us girls separated from sharing one bedroom, Josie got to move upstairs to the bungalow, leaving Leslie and me together. I did occasional spend time with Josie in that huge spacious area up there. As you walked up the stairs, there was a large library of books on a built-in shelf. Across from that were four walk-in closets. I loved all the space. Two large windows on each end of the room brought in tons of lighting. A queen-sized bed sat in the middle of the room with a plethora of movement available. Even though I was clear, my sister did not really want me around; I forced myself into her life. I tried to deliberately spend time with Josie in substitution for Mona. They were two completely different people though.

I was fascinated with Josie. She was a high school senior and a majorette in the band at Osborn. I often tried to twirl her baton after watching her do it effortlessly. My arms were not as long as Josie's, and that made it difficult to master. Although that was my sister's room now, it had been my mom's, and before that my parents. I wanted that bedroom for my own. At the age of six, I longed for solace. I began immersing myself into music. I listened to the Four Tops, Temptations, and anything Motown. The words to many of the songs fit my life to a tee. "Cloud Nine" was my favorite.

My middle siblings and I truly had no connections or bond during the formidable years. Henry and Leslie were in upper grade school and walking to the beat of their own drum. All of my early memories with them remain clouded in my mind, other than being in the bedroom with Leslie. Although certain things stand out for me, like being picked on, I do not recall ever having a lot of alone time with either of them.

Lunches in grade school were spent in the cafeteria. Leslie was old enough to go off school grounds, so one day she took me to a local sit-down burger joint only two blocks from the school, on Mound Road. It was very tiny, and Helen was the owner. Being with Leslie, I was not worried about getting back in time for class. Leslie and I sat at the counter with her friends, Donna and Beverly. Helen made the best-tasting hamburger I had ever eaten. Leslie got in big trouble from our school principal, Sister Virginia, when we returned from lunch. Apparently, it was against school policy for me to be off the grounds. I was suddenly afraid. I had such a good time hanging out with the older girls, now *I* was going to be in trouble. That proved to be a long-standing memory because I did not hang out with Leslie again, until *years* later. I additionally felt that I was to blame. Why though? That proved to be an ongoing feeling I had with me for decades. That was definitely a taught behavior.

My first-grade teacher, Sister Lanise, was a God sent to me. She instilled manners and respect into her students. Sister gave me hope for learning, and I loved her. Before attending school, while still at Aunt Kate's, I realized the world was not made up for people who were left-handed like me. Once I arrived in Sister Lanise's class, she pointed out to me several times to change the hand I was writing with. One particular day, while coloring an alphabet page, Sister said the devil was in my hand. She was quick to point out, with a ruler to my knuckles, that I needed to change my hand. I respectfully told her, "God wants me to use this hand." Sister Lanise never questioned me again; instead, she showed me how to write correctly. Sister listened to me, and most importantly, she validated me. I eventually came to realize something, a big something. I would never receive that from my family—validation!

I was a very inquisitive little girl and listened to Sr. Lanise all day, every day. She was a true authoritarian but also a very loving nun to me. I liked her strictness, and I never got into trouble. I just listened intently, doing as she asked. I soon began to stay after school to help her with chores. Cleaning the chalkboard first, I erased the last thing Sister had printed. I then took the erasers outside, two at a time, smacking them together. I made sure to get the chalk dusk from their folded felt layers. I repeated that task diligently, three times. Then I filled Sister's chalk ruler. It was an apparatus made from metal wire, controlled by a wooden handle. It held six long pieces of white chalk. Sister used it to make continuous lines on the chalkboard for our daily lessons.

I always helped to fix and decorate the large bulletin boards, which displayed our color pages and alphabet lesson. Sister Lanise kept a tidy classroom. I appreciated that about her. I can remember how I emotionally felt in first grade. I do not know if that is something another child experiences, but for me, it is very vivid. I can recall, with every experience I am about to share, all of my emotional feelings and mental thoughts. I did, after many years, come to understand what my mom meant when she repeatedly said "You wear your heart on your sleeve." Why yes, yes, I did.

Let Sexual Immortality and every sort of uncleanness or greediness not even be mentioned among you. Just as is proper for holy people. Neither shameful conduct nor foolish talk nor obscene justing—things that are not befitting—but rather the giving of thanks. For you know this recognizing for yourselves, that no sexually immoral person or unclean person or greedy person which means being an idolater has any inheritance in the kingdom of Christ and God.

—Ephesians 5:3–5

CHAPTER 3

At the age of seven, my life began to run a horrible course, one I never thought a child would encounter. They were situations a young mind should never have to contemplate. The events proved to be long-lasting and without punishment. These memories incapacitated me, molded me, and prevented my anger and resentment from being extinguished. Feelings of abandonment surfaced and remained for many, many years. My trust in others and the ability to say *no* would now be on a very naive level. The life I was about to embark upon was not good or healthy for anyone, especially a little girl.

I will preface the following by saying I have never been without God. He has walked with me through everything I have experienced. I have always kept my faith. I have at times been admittedly distant, believing I was not worthy of anything He had to offer. Over the years, however, God would prove to be a reckoning force, friend, and Father to me. It is very odd how memories are extremely vivid for something to have occurred years before, and yet the projector clearly runs the exact film reel verbatim in your head. It is quite remarkable.

I had three good friends whom I had met once I returned home: Joey, Marie, and Mary Jo. We all played together, having great fun. The neighborhood was very busy with children of all ages. My family was so large our ages spanned eleven years. Due to our size, my siblings knew a lot of people from in and around the neighborhood. Mary Jo had other siblings. Her older brother James was tall and lanky, with long stringy hair and was visually a hippy. James was always in trouble. He frequently stole their oldest sister's car, and the police would try to find it. Now I remind you, I had been home for less than a year. These were new people to me, and I was new to them.

One warm day, I remember skipping down the street to visit Mary Jo. She had a beautiful Mrs. Beasley doll, whom I adored. Mary Jo knew I loved playing with Mrs. Beasley and pulling her voice cord. I was so excited to be going to play with both of them. When I got to her house, James told me Mary Jo was in the backyard. I walked up the driveway; and there were approximately eight teenaged boys surrounding the garage and swimming pool. James coaxed me into the garage by saying Mary Jo was in there, and before I knew it, he shut the overhead door. He then cornered me and pulled his pants down. James had one hand on the wall above my left ear; the other hand was waiving his penis in my face and around my lips. His friends stood outside, peering through the window, laughing hysterically. On my right, the garage door was ajar. Large enough was the opening, my little body was able to squeeze out. I remember running down the street to go to my safe home. Those thirteen or so houses seemed like a mile's distance to me.

When I frantically ran through the front door, my mom was sitting at the dining room table. I will never forget that entire moment. I told her I had to speak to her privately. We went into the bathroom, she sat down on the toilet seat as I stood between her knees. I told my mom what happened to me. I remember the verbiage I used. I told her, "He waived his boy part in my face and around my mouth." She never comforted or consoled me. Instead, it was all that was ever mentioned, until about a week later. A lady, from Wayne County Social Services, came to the house to see me regarding what occurred. I explained everything to her, as I did to my mom. Then I waited and waited. It was swept under the rug. I wanted James to go to jail.

Nothing happened to James, and my mom *never* brought it up again. Mary Jo denied what occurred once social services paid her dad a visit. Our friendship was not strong any longer, although we continued to play together, very rarely. That, in itself, is very odd to me today. I began feeling I must not be too important to anyone after that occurred. I had many questions, and no one to answer them. I became sad, and confusion set into my mind.

I played in and around the neighborhood with Joey and Marie every day after school. Joey and I went to school together; he was a year younger than I. Marie went to a Lutheran School on Mound; she was a year younger than Joey. Mary Jo was the only one of us who attended public school at Van Zile. She one year older than me, the same age as my brother Danny. Mary Jo's dad was raising her because their mom had died. I remember seeing her mom once while she gardened on the side of their home.

On a particular morning, Joey's sister Donna, along with Joey, Leslie and I, walked to school. It had rained the night prior, so the sidewalks and streets had puddles. Joey tripped, falling onto the wet street. He was moments away from the sidewalk. Joey and I walked back to his house so he could change. We were late for school, but I had felt the need to walk back with him. Being there for Joey was more important to me than being tardy for school. Leslie and Donna walked to school ahead of us.

I was the type of girl who loved pleasing and helping other people. I enjoyed seeing them happy; it was a great feeling in my heart. Joey, Marie, and I had tea parties and played hopscotch and jacks. We loved using my front porch as a stage, singing together to our favorite songs. The three of us shared birthdays, and those parties together. We were great friends, and we were inseparable.

There were things we never spoke of, and situations within our families that were never discussed. Joey's mom and dad were alcoholics; he had two older sisters who went to school with two of my siblings. Marie had two older sisters also. We rarely saw them because they were grown and lived out of town. However, we knew Marie's sisters were from her mom's first marriage, which was unheard of in the early '70s. Each of us had our own issues, but no one identified with me. They had both of their parents living in their homes, taking care of them. That proved to be a lonely place for me emotionally.

Marie's dad was a stickler. He often made remarks about my household. Now mind you, I was very well-mannered. I never confronted an adult. Never. One day, Marie's dad took the three of us to his buddies to swim. I heard him gossiping with his friend about my dad. I knew anger, and I boiled over. I immediately exited the pool, went over to the table, and looked her dad in the eyes. I told him I was ready to go home. He knew—he knew I heard him. From that point on, I never cared for Marie's dad. He judged me because of my father's illness. That was unfair and not cool in my young mind.

The next year was challenging and quite painful for me. I did, in second grade, make my First Communion. I felt like a princess in my dress and veil. Even deeper, I felt I had reached a higher plateau within the church. Most importantly, I was bonded with God. Like many other girls my age, I felt a connection to becoming a sister of the church, a nun. That never stayed in my mind for long. I did not believe I was "sister" material. I believed I wanted to be a mom one day. I could not do that if I chose God as my husband.

The hard realities of my young life became more intense, and they had begun unraveling quickly. After making my communion, my mom took me to visit my dad so he could see me in my dress. My dad, at that time, was living at the YMCA in Detroit. I never knew why he was moved from Northville Mental Hospital. My mom and I walked up to the clerk at the desk and asked for my father. The tall man informed her my dad was in the Wayne County Jail. He had hit a man over the head with a skillet during an altercation, knocking him unconscious. My little heart was broken. My daddy, whom I did not see too frequently, was not there to see me in my communion dress. I even had my prayer book and rosary with me. I was beyond devastated.

On the trip back home, as we traveled down Mount Elliot Road, my mom never discussed the situation with me. I never knew how long my dad was in jail either. My mind said days, but I have no recollection. Upon making it home, I got undressed and retreated to my room. I was not bothered there; my mom never came in to check on me. I waited for her too. I wanted to hear her to tell me it would all be all right.

I prayed for my dad all the time. I wanted him so badly, and in a way that I thought was completely selfish. I was very explicit in my chats with God, praying boldly. I always asked for things *to come*, not the here and now. It was almost as if I had prayed as to set my future in God's book of good. I asked for a husband when I was old enough. I wanted his name to be Peter. He had to be a mechanic and love me through thick and thin. I often prayed for God to remove me from my born-into family. All I can say, God hears your prayers. He hears what is in your heart and in your soul.

The other, more dramatic event that forever changed my being was when my older brother Danny began molesting me. I was so small a girl. He was a year and seven months older than me. I do not recall how frequently the abuse occurred; however, it went on for years before coming to an end. Word of it was never spoken to another soul, other than to God. I kept it a secret for some twenty years, until becoming engaged to my husband. He was the only person I trusted with such an inner part of me. I never had the urge to tell my mom. After all, nothing happened to James. Why would Danny be any different? If anything, I thought by telling my mom, either Danny or I would be removed from the house. I imagined what could happen to me. Where would they put me? An orphanage? Or, even a more devastating scenario, nothing would happen, and I could remain in the home, becoming the hated child.

I had just gotten back to the family; I did not think I should have to leave again. It was my family, my home, and my new life. I attempted to tell Father Vernon in the confessional; however, he was not safe to me. He knew my whole family and had knowledge of our fraternal circumstances. I felt so violated and even tried to tell my grandparents, but they were very old-fashioned, and my mom's parents. They would not understand. I found myself in a predicament that was very uncomfortable in my soul. I am so sad for that little girl today. She had no one to turn to and no one to go to.

One occasion, I remember very well. Leslie was upstairs wrapping Christmas gifts, and I ran to her for help. Danny had cornered me in the boy's bedroom and refused to let me go. He did bad things to me when the house was empty, but Leslie was home. I was confused, my breath heavy once I reached the top of the stairs. I did not even care that the packages said *To Barbara, From Santa*. What? No Santa? In my mind, that did not even faze me. I went up there for help, but instead I froze. I was totally frozen! I wanted the molestation to stop but was too afraid to tell Leslie what had just occurred. I knew in my heart Danny should not be doing these things to me. I knew it was wrong of him and it felt so disgusting. The pressure, that I had no voice, overwhelmed and overpowered my young mind.

I believe at some point in time, Danny bragged to his friends in the neighborhood of what he was able to get away with. I say that is a belief after having thought of it over the years. Those boys were slick. They ended up enticing me to "play" with them, using toys to lure me. Danny was not that way though. He was demanding and mean, many times making me go to the basement and lay on the pool table. There he orally molested me, making me do the same to him. I thank God all the time for my having only been penetrated by his finger. It would take years of guilt, plus a mind overwhelmed with anxiety, to overcome those feelings.

I felt dirty and nasty every time Danny touched me. He was masterfully sickening in his approach. He threatened me on many occasions. I wanted to be protected so badly but had no one to turn to. For many years, I blocked those thoughts out. As a child, I never felt I was equipped to make it stop. I never knew how, plus there was no safe person to go to for help. At the time of the abuse, I would escape to Mary Jo's to play with Mrs. Beasley. If that was not an option, I went to my secret hideout. There I would sit for what seemed like the whole day, and I prayed. I never questioned God. I was taught to never question authority of any type, and God was my utmost authority. He was, and is, my Father. I just prayed!

Any positive feelings I had about myself were nearly diminished. I did not feel good; I felt impure and nasty. Even though I never blamed myself for what Danny did to me, I held my mind accountable and hostage for years, during and after the abuse. The abuse itself never ended; it just changed into a different kind of manipulation, intimidation, and bullying.

Two years later, my mom, Danny, and I went to Camp Metamora Park for a summer afternoon. We met many other people there, for a day of fishing and hiking, fun and exploration. The song "Flashlight" by Parliament was playing on the radio as a popular hit. That was the summer the sexual assaults stopped. I was going on eleven. No longer sexually assaulted; I was now a target of his extreme anger, along with verbal, mental, and physical abuse.

Danny and I fought a lot. On occasion, the fighting escalated into knockdowns, drag-outs, and altercations. My mom watched as we physically punched and shoved each other in the hallway of our house. I never knew why he beat me up; I was a peaceful girl. I longed for quietness and love. Those were two things that would never be obtainable with my born-into family. Danny was a hard-core bully in my eyes. I wondered why my mom never intervened. Being she did not, I felt compelled to defend myself. That was my earliest recollection for the onset of name-calling. I, from that point on, referred to Danny as a "sissy." He hated that name. Danny thought of himself as big and bad, and that is the persona he gave off. I began to wonder if he missed my dad too.

After the fights, I would run out the door and down the block. There was a Greek Orthodox Church on Mound and Emery. I hid in the front of the church, creeping down to the basements window's edge. From the street level, you could not see my spot. It was a deep step, and I would jump down into it. I came across my hideout while walking home from school. No one ever found me there because of the two giant bushes covering the front. I frequented that quiet location a lot. It was my personal secret.

One evening, it was dark outside, and Danny was harassing me in the front room. He pushed me too far that night; I had enough. He had me by my hair, pulling it tightly, not allowing me to defend myself. Finally getting the perfect opportunity, I kicked him between the legs, watching him fall quickly to the ground. Inside of my heart, I was so happy I had defended myself. My mom was screaming at me. *"Don't you know, you never kick a boy there?"* What? "What about me, Mom?" I sadly cried.

I ran out of the house and headed to my hideout. I could feel someone behind me as I reached the middle of the block. Danny was following me. *He is never going to find my hiding spot*, I thought. So I made a detour and went on the next block and walked. Another question I could never get an answer to was why in the world did Danny follow me after beating on me? I had concluded he was going to attack me. Maybe leave me for dead!

I have affection for you, O God, my strength. God is my crag and my stronghold and the one who rescues me. My God is my rock, in whom I will take refuge, my shield and my horn of salvation, my secure refuge. I call on God who is worthy of praise, and I will be saved from my enemies.
—Psalms 18:1–3

CHAPTER 4

I vividly remember lying on my bed, crying for my daddy to help me, as a young girl. I somehow thought he was going to be my savior, but he never came. During those emotional times, my sister Leslie would scream out to me, "Shut up, he's not coming for you!" Then she would laugh. That was traumatic for me. I frequently napped during those days, to pass my time after such an ordeal. Sleeping or leaving the house helped me to temporarily not think about it anymore.

I thought—even though I was made to believe differently—my dad, was in fact, rescuing me from my born-into-family's hatred. I imagined him as an angel coming to save me. That never happened. It appeared to me I was continuously being put in bad situations. I wore straightjackets that no one could help me escape. I felt like I was caught in a net, just like a fish, but no fisherman was there to pull me out. There was no one to go to.

I frequently went to the school park to play on the wooden swings. It was six blocks to walk, one that I always enjoyed. I had stops on the way every time I took a particular route. I never missed an opportunity to feel the pussy willow trees that stood on the side of the Greek Orthodox Church as I walked down Emery. They were so soft and felt great against my cheeks as I stroked each side of my face, lips, and forehead.

Other times, I walked straight down Syracuse to stop and visit Mr. Frank. He owned the dry cleaners on the corner of 7 Mile. Mr. Frank was a thin black man who never treated me as a child bothering him. He and I became quick friends. The inside of the building was very steamy, and had the distinct odor found in cleaners. Mr. Frank was a funny man who constantly had a smile on his face. He and I talked real talk and spent a lot of time together. I was able to carry on conversations with older folks because of the Kay's. He asked me how I felt about certain things that were going on in the world. Mr. Frank was a warm soul and a cool cat.

One day, I made my way down to the park. I saw Henry, smoking cigarettes behind the utility building with a friend. I asked him about it when he got home, telling him I did not want him to die from smoking. He told me if I said "anything to Mom"; he would have to tell her I was smoking too. So, I told my mom the whole story. Henry, as I recall, was not directly mad at me, but he did take it out on my homework. I laugh and smile now as I think of it, but at the time, my mouth dropped open at what he had done. Henry decided to take the spelling words I had to memorize, and he changed many of the words into swear words. For instance, *cute*, *shirt*, and *ask* became words that were not approved of. Yes, I know!

Henry was not vindictive; he just thought he was funny. He treated me cordially, and never set out to hurt me in any way. Henry and I were not necessarily close, but I really liked him because he never gave me flak. He was around the house more than John, so we often played. He was very quiet by nature and did not say too much as a rule. Henry was funny though, and I did not have a lot of laughter in my life. I recall quite a few times getting "Indian burns" on my wrists, "tickle treatments" until I cried, and "noogies" on my head. Henry always played with me, never harassing my spirit.

One night, the Lipinski's had a party in their father's basement. I was walking down Dwyer with Joey when Henry told us to go inside and head downstairs. We did. It was the first time I drank alcohol. Someone offered me a rum and coke, and I remember sucking that down like pop. It was so good; I was eleven.

About that time in the household, things would take a horrible turn. John, my oldest brother, went to Derby Hill, our local park, after drinking whiskey all night long. There, he attempted to commit suicide by cutting his wrist. He had three friends whom he always hung out with: Rick, Vince, and Rusty. I wondered where they were since they were always inseparable. John went away after that. Not knowing where he was, I prayed for him continuously. He did come home eventually, but it was months later. I never found out where he went. When John returned, he had a gift for me.

It was a small green box that was hinged; it was lined with felt. John made it for me while he was gone, and I cherished it. I used it for a small jewelry box, putting my beloved picture of Mikhail Baryshnikov on the bottom.

That same summer, while John was away, Lynn was chasing Henry around the house, inside and out. I began to realize she was flirting with Henry. Lynn ran through the front door, slamming it behind her. Henry's arm went right through the glass. There was blood everywhere, and Henry's upper arm was shredded. Our neighbor came to help us, and I stayed to assist. We wrapped his arm up, putting pressure on it, and then he was rushed to Holy Cross Hospital. My mom was called off the line at Chrysler, and she came home immediately. I did, in my young mind, wonder if she would have done the same for me. Henry ended up with a massive scar on his arm. Lynn knew she was responsible, but never apologized. That was so wrong.

I had many thoughts running through my head. I did not feel any child should go through what I was enduring. I was never protected, embraced, or cared for, except by my grandparents and the Kays. I wondered if God would answer my prayers. I do want to clarify the fact; I did think my mom loved me, because she told me she did. However, as an adult, I learned simply saying the words does not make it factual. It is not enough to say the words if words are all you get. You must have a positive action to support the love. If you are constantly being put down, ridiculed, or degraded as I was, that is *not* love, that is resentment. I, as an adult, can rationalize that; but as a child, I could not.

John and Henry were good to me the majority of the time. However, the only thing that distracted them was hockey. All three of my brothers loved the sport. They watched, played, and breathed it. My Auntie Rosie had given me a gorgeous doll for my birthday. I had her a whole two weeks before she was destroyed. It was a conspiracy on my brother's end, to kill my doll. They tore the head off of her and wrapped it in black hockey tape. I looked everywhere for her, even asking them if they had seen her. They unanimously said no. But when I was perched upon the landing at the bottom of the steps, I watched them take shots in the basement. It took me a few minutes to realize their puck was round. I questioned them, and they busted into laughter. I knew what they had done, and I marched upstairs to inform my mom.

Instead of being comforted, my mom was cooking and told me to "get out of the kitchen." I cried, explaining what they had done. It may be comical reading of the encounter; however, living it was horrible. My mom, instead of scolding them, disciplined me. I just did not understand.

> Continue being merciful, just as your father is merciful.
> —Luke 6:36

CHAPTER 5

Out of the six children, I was definitely the one who saw my father the most. As my dad got moved from place to place, often living in different types of facilities, I always went with my mom to visit him. The frequency of our visits was monthly, sometimes biweekly. My mom brought him a huge canister of pipe tobacco, snacks, and clean clothes on nearly every occasion we went.

I loved my dad and really looked forward to his big hugs and kisses. Till today, I can still smell his cherry tobacco. He was very handsome, and the fact that he smoked a pipe was so debonair to me. There were many things I analyzed about my dad. I watched his facial expressions, the tone of his voice, and especially the way he and my mom interacted. I easily picked up on how my dad was feeling on particular days. His face spoke without the use of his vocal cords. Sometimes my dad was sad to see me. I prayed for him daily and every night before sleeping. I prayed for him to get better and be a father to me. The mannerisms of my mom were cold and non-loving toward him. I could not even fathom the two of them together. My mom was standoffish and seemingly there, only out of obligation.

I came to realize my mom did that with many things. My dad was just one example. There were vows said "in sickness and in health" that my mom obviously forgot about. She did not *help* my dad in any way to get *better*. I wondered if my mom prayed for my dad the way she said she prayed for us kids. I witnessed my mom "disown" him, and it seemed effortless for her.

On more than one occasion, my mom had a coworker come to our home. His name was Lonnie Wood, and he also worked for Chrysler. I investigated the back driveway from both of my bedroom windows. That was where he parked his car. The windows were steamy, and I was no dummy. One thing I did possess that no one could steal from me was street smarts.

My dad and I built a great relationship over time. Kind and loving, just detached from reality. I remember going to a restaurant with my parents during one visit. My dad was a draftsman in his career, which today is similar to an engineer/graphic designer. He was extremely talented, and even designed the headlights for a Ford Mustang during his short career in the '60s. That afternoon, my dad sketched out a picture for me on a napkin. He began with drafting lines, and then he proceeded to make a clown on the paper. My dad was exact in his drawing and articulately detailed. I still have that napkin. The clown signified something to him, perhaps happier, carefree times.

On one occasion, my dad hopped on a bus and came home. My mom was livid. She felt my father should not be heard of until she went to visit him. My dad had been medically labeled Paranoid Schizophrenic since my brother Henry was one. That was in 1962, when he was diagnosed. My whole life, I never knew my dad to be in our house. Upon coming home from playing, I saw him in the living room. He had taken the bus and once he arrived, my dad felt the need to *fix* a working furnace. I distinctly remember my mom being so frantic. Her intuition told her my dad had "broken" or "tampered" with it. I can still hear her saying "The house can blow up." I remember praying to God for the house to be okay. My mom had to pay for a professional to come and inspect our furnace that day. Then, all of a sudden, my dad never came around any longer. Ever! I recall my mom was very upset at having to pay out money for the inspection.

As an only child, my dad lost both parents in 1956, ten years before I was born. They died three months apart from one another. Grandpa Lee worked in a steel mill as a general steel worker, and died from cirrhosis of the liver. Grandma Anita was a nurse's assistant at Holy Cross Hospital on Outer Drive. She contracted Hepatitis C from blood she had handled. The stories that came from my mom indicated my grandparents were not attentive to my dad's needs while he was maturing and coming of age. When my father was eight, my grandma and grandpa went to the bar, leaving him inside the car to wait for their return. My dad had many struggles growing up, only to become ill at twenty-five years old. There are many professionals who will tell you the onset of mental illness usually happens because something traumatic triggers it. The change in personality is created by a chemical imbalance. I surmise it was the death my grandparents and Josie's birth that sent his mental being into a tailspin.

My grandparents never saw my dad's illness once he had been diagnosed. They both passed away. I would love to share more of the heritage from my dad's family in this book; however, that is all I know. The things my great-uncle spewed from his lips indicated there was much more to their story. He stated to my mom, "Let the skeletons remain in the closet." In my inquisitive mind, that never sat well with me. It became apparent in my thinking that mental illness ran rampant in their family. I also found out through some research, my grandfather and his brothers were all heavy alcoholics. Many times, people who suffer from mental illness also have a crutch or habit. That is referred to as a co-concurring illness.

When my dad first got ill, and my mom did not know what was happening, she went to my dad's uncle. He was Grandpa Lee's brother, great-uncle Jimmy. At the meeting, my mom was told to "mind your own business," and "not stir up the past." *What the hell does that mean?* may have been her reaction to that comment; I do not know. But her action was to do nothing. From that point on, my great-uncle and great-aunt no longer had anything to do with my dad, my mom, or the kids who were born into that union. My mom handled the diagnosis unsuccessfully, and listened to the doctors exclusively.

As I grew up, people asked about my dad. I uninhibitedly said, "My dad doesn't live with us, he's paranoid schizophrenic." I did not even know the totality of the statement. I heard my mom say it all the time, but I was not the type of girl to have fear. Everyone on my street knew, and soon my classmates learned of it. "How?" they asked, and I would say the above phrase, not being ashamed in any way. My mom said things like "Keep your mouth shut" and "What goes on in this house, stays in this house," or "What the hell are you doing broadcasting our business with that big mouth of yours?" That puzzled me, because I was not ashamed of my dad being ill. I was a child and did not know the stigma attached to mental illness. I would still be very open with whomever asked. It was, after all, who I was. I was being true to myself at the time and never even knew it. I was constantly told I was different and to act "normally." I liked being unique, and for the most part, I liked my personality. I enjoyed talking, it made me feel better; I just did not have anyone to share my voice with.

As a child, many thoughts permeated my mind as to how I came to be born. If my dad became ill in 1962 how was it that Danny and I were born? I saw the relationship between my parents, and I knew instinctively it was not strong. After all, my mom gave absolutely no affection to my dad. She never hugged or kissed him when we visited. If you created six children with a man, I expected affection to be had. No, not from my mom.

I was an inquisitive child and very overt in my questions, so I asked my mom if I was born to her. Many times, my siblings told me my mom bought me at Kmart and I had popped out of a toaster. They said she felt sorry for me and took me home. My mom's explanation to me was "All your dad had to do was hang his pants on the bedpost and I'd be pregnant." As a result, Danny and I were born. I was young but felt it was an inappropriate comment, one I did not fully understand. I grew to see my mom never wanted more children after Henry.

Like many other conversations between my mom and I, that one did not sit well within my spirit. My mom lacked tact. After listening to her explain the story, I began to feel she never wanted me. I felt I was an accident following that uncomfortable conversation. Those feelings stayed with me for a long time, many, many years. They were horrible visions, feelings, and memories. I somehow was aware, though, one day I would need the tools to learn how to overcome the obvious detachment of my own mother's heart.

In my mind, a child should be tenderly loved and showered with goodness. I was not. I do not believe I am an accident today. I believe I am a gift from God with a divine destiny in front of me, in the area of helping others. We are not our upbringing or our childhood. Occasionally, we as human beings feel that statement is true, but it is not. It is so very important to follow your instincts when it comes to building your own character. You can choose to be anything you want. Anything! Parents often cause damage to minds and hearts. We must pull ourselves up, continuing to move forward, in lieu of our circumstances. I observed my mom after her explanation about my being born. I was not treated any differently by her per say, but things were different.

My mom was an outspoken factory worker who never complained about her life, just others. I believe—and stand firm on the fact—my mom raised us to be racist, with a character to judge others. Like other things she did, that most definitely never sat well within my spirit. My mom was in the business of talking about others, however, never improving herself. I had many friends and never paid attention to their skin color. I did, of course, know their nationalities; however, I never called anyone "colored" or referred to black folks in a very racist way, as my mom did. My mom and I were total opposites. I liked my friends for how they played with me. If I did not like how I was being treated, they simply were no longer a part of my circle.

I never judged people on anything, other than how they acted toward me and others. How could that be? My entire household seemed racist, so how was I different? I came to question God. I asked him multiple times if I was born into the wrong family. My answer was always a resounding *no. I was here to learn* was the message I received. Working in a factory, my mom complained about the black people smoking weed and drinking alcohol at lunch. Then she said, "They're coming back to work, supposedly to build quality cars?" My mom made comments about how *they* were not following the rules of the union. She went on and on about how she "has to pay her union dues, and that means you are there to be a good worker." I realized a lot at that time!

My mom did not like black people because of work. She categorized the whole race as being lazy, drug addicts, and drunkards. I loved my mom because she was my mom, but from that day on, I knew she was a racist, and that was not right. I never felt I had any power, so how could I tell her she was wrong? I was very different in my thinking from that of any other sibling, and I knew it instinctively. I knew many things instinctively. I firmly feel that is why I never felt as if I *fit in* with my born-into family. I think they saw something different in my soul, and for whatever reason, they did not like it. My mom raised us to be racist! I believe she set out to teach us in that manner, because she never held her tongue. It was a hard fact for my mind to wrap around. I knew what kind of person I was, and a racist was definitely not it. I was loving and kind, giving and helpful. I could never hate a race of people. Besides, the only people I did not like were the ones hurting me.

> Lying lips are detestable to God, but those acting
> faithfully bring pleasure to him.
>
> —Proverbs 12:22

CHAPTER 6

When I was nine, my mom's good friend Karen and she went out for an evening. My mom met a man that particular night while she and Ms. Karen were at a bar. It is ironic, since the gentleman and my mom were not drinkers. They were simply there with friends. Steven was tall and very good-looking. He was a Polish Catholic divorcee, and it was easy to see my mom's attraction to him. He had a deep voice, but it was soft. Steve would become, in so many ways, a savior for my mom. I am a firm believer God brings others into our lives with a purpose behind it. The same holds true to those who are removed. In the beginning of their relationship, it was a definite adjustment for every one of us. I really did not like the idea that my mom was married to my dad and dating.

Of course, the reality of my father returning to our house was not even in the equation, and at this time, my mom was forty-two years old. My mom often made it clear she would stay married until everyone of us had graduated high school. I no longer thought my dad was coming home to be a real dad to me. Leslie made sure of that. I never saw my mom date. Lonnie Wood was not dating my mom if he was parking his car in the yard. I think he was sneaking around. Maybe he was married? I could only imagine, because we were never introduced to him.

My meeting Steve for the first time is embedded in my head. I was sitting on a wooden log John made into a seat. He had shellacked it to seal the wood, and I often sat there next to the fireplace. Steve walked in the front door, standing in the vestibule. He graciously introduced himself to all of us who were still living at home. I looked up at that bigger-than-life man and asked if he was going to be my new dad. He laughed and said, "No, you only have one dad." That was a good enough explanation to me.

Steve was a very kind and gentle soul. He paid attention to me in a friendly manner. As he had, on more than one occasion said, "I'm not here to be your dad, I just want to teach you what I know, as a friend." He did that too. I had quite a bit of leeway with Steve. He was very generous and kind to me. Steve lived on 8 Mile and Dequindre in a trailer. He was in those circumstances due to a divorce. Steve, like my mom, worked for Chrysler. As the years progressed, he proved to be quite a comrade to me.

Over time, my mom and Steve built a happy and strong relationship, eventually falling in love. I had eight more years before graduating from high school; I had plenty of time to get to know him. I never imagined what a wonderful human being he would turn out to be. No one else was thrilled for my mom. Danny overtly resented Steve. Henry and Leslie could take him or leave him. I liked him thus far. Also, I did not want my mom to be alone.

Steve had five children. He had a daughter who was a year younger than me. I met her one day after school when Steve dropped her off. He thought I could meet her and that we would enjoy playing with one another. Her name was Cara. She looked just like her dad and had a very warm smile. My mom was driving down the block, coming home from work. She stopped the car in the middle of the street while Cara and I were walking. She had a scowl on her face, asking who the girl was. Once I told my mom, "Steve's daughter, Cara." She changed her entire mannerism. My mom gave a smile that was totally fake. Her voice changed into a sweet demeanor.

I could not understand that as a child, but as an aware adult, it is an eye-opener. I never noticed that trait in my mom before, the fake voice. Only Josie did that to gain attention from boys and men. It seemed so plain to just be me, but I liked who I was. My born-into family did their best to try to change me into one of them. After that occurrence with Cara, I became more aware of my surroundings and my place within the family.

Over a period of years, Steve began reading books on investment and self-help. His favorite author was Dr. Wayne Dyer. He had a cassette tape of Dr. Dyer's, which I had the privilege of listening to. I never thumbed through the books Steve had, but I was always drawn to them. I watched him closely and listened intently as he schooled me. He laughed a lot, mixing humor into real life experiences. I appreciated him for that. I had never gotten that type of male affection before. It was truly refreshing and very welcoming. I was finally getting the love I had longed for, and I believe Steve was getting the same since he had not received any from his children. I missed Uncle Ian less and less now.

My family laughed infrequently. The only memories I have of laughing were with my cousins, or while watching TV. Perhaps at Belle-Air drive-in theater. The times were few and far between, and that meant something as an adult. I recall watching the Carol Burnett Show or Flip Wilson with Henry. We both cracked up. That was a release for me. My mom seldom smiled. I knew she had a lot going on, but I could not understand why she was so rigid and uptight.

Steve loved my cheeks, and he always called me "little gerbil" or "gerbil cheeks." I honestly hated that. I felt it was an insult of sorts. He laughed at my anger, which made me resent him a bit. I was not mean to Steve, but became quiet and withdrawn. At times, I became very angry, never understanding why. I still prayed every night and during the days. I considered myself a good girl who never got into any real trouble.

Steve tried to build me up, looking back. I think he was trying to help make me feel pretty and wanted. I did eventually feel love for myself, because he did his job! I felt pretty, but no one treated me as if I were; therefore, I had not gained the confidence I needed. Looking back on the life Steve had, I see now how strong a man he truly was. Steve was a fighter, I believed. So, I watched, observed, and learned. He was an alcoholic in his former life and had now been in recovery for many years. My mom had mentioned that once in passing, because they had met in a bar.

Steve never acted like Joey's parents, and those were the only alcoholics I was around, other than the Samanski's on the corner. Steve was in control all the time, and I always admired that. I came to realize what Alcoholic Anonymous was all about, and I was intrigued. He saw that alcohol destroyed his family life, and he did not want that again. Steve was both physically and emotionally very capable.

The new man in my mom's life was making all kinds of waves in the house. Henry and Danny said they would never listen to him, because he was not their dad. Leslie was only concerned with her friends, skipping school and getting high on weed. She often openly rolled it in front of me. She smoked upstairs in the bungalow while my mom was at work.

Josie and John had already moved out. I personally did not understand everyone's blasé attitude. I loved having a man in the home on weekends. Steve always made me comfortable.

While working afternoons, Steve decided to get a dog for companionship. He named him Lonesome, meaning Steve had to leave the radio on for the dog when he went to work. I loved Lonesome; I had never been around a dog in a playful way. He lived with Steve at his trailer, in order to be a watchdog. It did not take long before it became apparent; Lonesome was unable to continue living there. He had no stimulation during the day while Steve slept, or in the evenings when he worked. It was too much alone time for a puppy.

I became so excited because my born-into family finally got a dog. Lonesome was so playful and loving. The only downside was none of us knew anything about taking care of a dog. Cats, yes; dogs, absolutely not. He was not disciplined consistently for puppy behavior. Lonesome was yelled at, as if he knew better. My siblings treated him like he was in the way. Danny was very mean, often kicking Lonesome. I hated that and always gave the puppy extra lovin'. I never liked Danny; I only learned to quietly tolerate him.

Now we had Lonesome the dog and Tabby the cat living in our home. Tabby was a gift from God. Found as a stray in my neighbor Mr. Gaines's front yard, I quickly scooped him up, claiming him as mine. I asked my mom if I could keep him, and she agreed. The only stipulation was that I had to care for Tabby as my own. So I did just that. Tabby and I became the best of friends. He slept with me and licked my tears when I cried. I cried a lot too. He was fun and playful; I loved him dearly. I believe both Tabby and Lonesome *were* brought to me as *therapy animals* by God. They came to me at a low time in my life. Those animals brought comfort and unconditional love when my world was upside down. Their unselfish souls remained in my life for many years, never wavering in their companionship.

From early on, I had an undeniable kindship with animals. My mom never brought one to us though, and I was the only one bringing in strays. I fed them and gave all my love to them. I had another cat come to me as a kitten. Monkey and I bonded quickly with one other. He often nibbled on my earlobes, waking me up in the mornings for school. I found him in the alley and buried him there during Christmas break that same year.

Lonesome was a wonderful and playful puppy. He only wanted to play with Monkey, but instead bit him so forcefully; Monkey died from his injuries. I was devastated, and it was then that I knew total sadness.

I resented Lonesome and yelled at him, sometimes hitting his nose. I hate myself and those memories. How could you love something so much, taking care of their every need, and then hit them? Well, I was a product of a dysfunctional household. I forgave Lonesome quickly, realizing it was an accident; and we remained great pals. I wish I had only learned to forgive myself sooner, but that would take me some twenty-five years to get over.

> There is nothing better for a man to eat and drink and find enjoyment in his hard work. This too, I have realized is from the hand of God.
> —Ecclesiastes 2:24

CHAPTER 7

Marie and I began taking ballet together. We practiced inside the Activities Building, which sat between my church and school. Mrs. Nickie was our instructor, and she also taught tap and jazz dancing. I loved classical music, thanks to Mona and Josie, so taking ballet classes made me ecstatic. Chopin, Copland, and Vivaldi were my favorites. Marie and I got a ride from her dad at 8:30 every Saturday morning. Sometimes, we snuck into the kitchen of the Activities Building after lessons, and took full-sized candy bars from the freezer. While walking home, we devoured them. Dancing and music were definitely releases or escapes for me.

I loved Mrs. Nickie. Her attitude was loving, compassionate, caring, and structured. Mrs. Nickie not only encouraged me; she taught me how to be a lady. She was a fine dance instructor, always putting events on in the Activities Building at the end of summer. We never went a year without the dancers, chipping in to buy her a huge bouquet of flowers. At the close of the performance, she was presented with them. It was my job to purchase the arrangement, taking special care to pack it with love. I felt doing that was a great responsibility and an internal reward.

In addition to ballet, I also took tap and jazz. I learned grace, rhythm, and timing. I was not shy, and my wonderful mentor and teacher knew my personality was outgoing yet guarded. Mrs. Nickie was abreast of my overtness and welcomed it. It was okay to be myself in front of her and in her dance classes. That was a welcoming feeling to experience. I also had Mrs. Nickie as an art teacher during school. She again amazed me with her talents. I really looked up to her as a woman role model. I had always prayed after Mrs. Nickie left St. Louis the King, that God would bring her back into my life. I wanted to tell her what an inspiration she had been to me during the dark times of my childhood.

In the same time frame, I had a girlfriend whose grandmother lived on Dwyer. Michelle stayed after school with her grandma every day until her mom picked her up. She and I played outside together after classes. On the weekends, her grandmother cleaned the inside of the church the old-fashioned Polish way. She would polish the pews, mop the floors, and then scrub the bathrooms and sanctuary down. I remember Michelle's grandma using Pine Sole to clean those areas. I have loving flashbacks when I smell that cleaning product today. Michelle's grandma, on occasion, let us help. I was an extraordinary cleaner, her grandma told me so.

I also had a small job at the local beauty shop when I was ten years old. The salon was across the street from our church. I walked into the parlor one Saturday morning, asking Estell if she needed any help. From there on, I had a job. I used Spic and Span on the floors, washing them with a mop. I quickly realized why my grandma never used mops. All they honestly did was move dirt around, building it up in the corners, and never truly cleaning well. Once that happened, and the wax was applied, you could forget about ever getting the dirt up again, unless it was scrapped off.

I had jovial and outgoing personalities around me some of the time. They may have been parents of friends, teachers, priests, or just me and the circumstances I created to entertain myself. That is where I got my humor from. Sarcastic? At times, but funny! I never got that at home. Humor was not shown in my house at any time. I remember being happy a lot of the time despite my young tribulations. Joey and Marie were my life. The three of us did so much adventuring together. Joey and I shared a love of rock 'n' roll. His all-time favorite bands were Kiss and Heart. I gravitated only toward one artist as my favorite: Peter Frampton. However, I loved all classic rock 'n' roll and Motown. I was very fortunate, with my love of music, to have grown up at such a pivotal time in history.

In the summer of 1976, Joey and I both got permission from our parents to go to Pine Knob Music Theater. We were going to see Frampton Live. It was huge for both of us, and our first time attending a live concert. I loved Frampton's music so much, and even more, the rhythms and words spoke to me. My all-time favorites were "Penny for Your Thoughts" and

"Baby I Love Your Ways." What a fantastic experience it was, hearing that in a live venue.

Frampton was an escape for me. I had originally gotten the *Frampton Comes Alive* album from my neighbor Mandy, but only to borrow. Once I got it home, and I opened up the full-sized album cover—*bam!*—out fell one of two albums onto the floor, breaking off a corner. I was devastated because Mandy was nice enough to lend me the record to begin with, and I knew it was expensive. I told my mom, and she and I went to the Musicland that day and bought a brand-new album. I explained what happened; Mandy understood and thanked me for replacing it. Now that I had broken Mandy's album, the original was mine to keep. I played that record every day. Every night, I put it on my turntable, playing it until I was ready to fall asleep. I had a connection to music early on, thanks to Mona. I loved the way the words came to life. It was a great escape for me mentally.

I suppose you could say I made my own fun. I did things that would and would not have gained approval from my mom. Nothing horrible, just kids having fun. For instance, Joey and I frequently walked to Hardee's Restaurant on 8 Mile and Mound for pop. We sat in the back of the restaurant and made spit balls from our straw wrappers. Then we proceeded to spit them onto the ceiling with our straws. We were banned from there after getting caught. I recall laughing the entire walk home.

We also used to walk down the alley and wreck the mean neighbor's flowers. One older lady, in particular, was very rude and crabby to us. We perused the fence, picking her snapdragons that lined the back of her property. She would give us the stink-eye every time she saw us. I think she knew. To me though, it became uncool to do that. I knew firsthand the amount of work they took in planting, let alone waiting for the blooms. Those were the most malicious things we did. Truth be told, we helped, and we were friends to many seniors in our neighborhood. The ones standing out gave us encouragement, love, and cookies, or homemade bread. They taught us, without us even knowing it.

There was Martha and her husband, John. They lived on our block, about ten houses south of me and kitty corner from Joey. We spent many summer mornings and afternoons helping them. We weeded their flower gardens in the backyard and pulled the weeds out from the cracks in the driveway. I had tons of experience for a young girl. After all, I did these jobs for Aunt Kate. When done working for John and Martha, we got paid with a can of Faygo pop and some kind of snack, usually M&M chocolate or a bag of Better Made chips. The rewards were yummy and fun. We also went down to their basement and played pinball. John was so gentle and kindhearted. He collected pinball machines and had many to choose from. Joey enjoyed that end of the *pay* for helping out; my enjoyment were the sweets.

I have loving memories of Grandma and Grandpa B, my adopted grandparents. They were in their late seventies, and their home was on the next block, on Albany off of Lantz. Nearly every day after school, Joey and I stopped at their house for cookies and milk. We all chatted about our day. Grandpa sat in the front room, while Grandma, Joey, and I stayed in the kitchen. I used to think grandpa was not listening to us, but then he chimed in with a question or comment. Grandma was a very tidy lady. Her home always had a certain scent when I walked in. It was very cozy, warm, and welcoming.

Mr. Holter was another neighbor. He lived with his longtime sweetheart, and they were in their seventies. Mr. Holter had four o' clocks on the south side of his house. Every day, around dinner time, the well-manicured bushes bloomed. They opened up so gingerly, and then they closed tightly, sometime during the night. The colors were glorious to me. My mom said Mr. Holter and his sweetie never got married because they stood to lose their individual social security. It never even seemed to me that my mom knew them, yet she told me about their lives. I wondered about how that came to be.

Grandma Berry was old and sweet. The cookies that came from her kitchen were gooey and delicious, and the majority of the time, they were warm. I would knock on her side door, and she joyfully gave them out. She was on the opposite corner from my house, on Outer Drive, facing Derby Hill. Grandma Berry was in her eighties. She weeded her own yard, raking, sweeping, and mowing, always staying active. I often asked her to allow me to assist her in gardening, but she always declined. What a wonderful teacher to watch in action. I learned from Grandma Berry that movement at any age was imperative in staying young.

I could never leave Mr. Frank out. After years of visiting him through the fence of the alley, Joey and I got invited into his home. Mr. Frank was a widowed man who lived on Outer Drive also. He made homemade bread all of the time, and it seemed like I smelled that freshness on a daily basis. The aroma, from the baking bread, was outstanding. Mr. Frank, on this particular day, began to instruct us on how the bread was made. Step by step. As we walked up into the kitchen, he had a loaf in the oven, one in a pan with a towel over it and a pile of flour on his counter. Mr. Frank was a true baker in my eyes.

He began performing the steps involved in getting the pile of flour into a loaf. He had just removed one from the oven and it was piping hot. The aroma was so much better in person, then from my driveway. Mr. Frank told us that the loaf had to sit for a half an hour. We began listening carefully and watched attentively as the next bowl became another loaf. Then we began viewing the process from the beginning. The flour was kneaded and then it was put into a bowl for some extremely lengthy time, in my eyes. Once that process was complete, the three of us enjoyed the first that had cooled. I still smell that dough baking. The bread my mom bought in Hamtramck was tasty; but Mr. Frank's was amazing. He was a very loving and giving man after that encounter. It was my first and last time in his home.

Inspirational people do not teach for recognition. They teach because it is in their hearts to do so. Many times, they will never know the impact they have had on us as children. I was fortunate that with all the ugly children and adults in my past, I continued to be blessed by outside people who genuinely cared and ultimately did inspire me. Even though bad things occurred to me as a child, every day events such as the ones I had with the neighbors mentioned above truly aided in my growth. They taught me to be kind, how to love and respect my fellow man, and that working hard has a great payoff, be it pulling weeds for a bag of chips or making bread for simply a slice. I also learned that older people have tons of wisdom to share, if only we listened.

I had a huge family in my eyes, all those sisters and brothers to teach me like Mona did. That was my initial belief, sticking to that way of thinking, for many years to come. I did not know why, but I constantly felt lonely and abandoned. That feeling was a deep, internal loneliness, not the kind that requires a person around you. It was a feeling I knew I was entitled to in my heart and soul, yet never received. My family never taught me the valuable lessons I learned. I was taught by outsiders. I calculated over the years the helpful lessons my mom gave to me. There was not much to add up.

My mom, I was constantly told, worked very hard on the assembly line at Chrysler. I observed her daily when she arrived home; her face and limbs, always long and tired. My mom's main concern, and her goals, consisted of raising her six children to be Christian adults with morals and values. We needed be hardworking and upstanding people. We were ultimately responsible for making her look, as if she has done a full and complete job raising us. All of us were expected to provide for ourselves. We were taught never to ask for handouts, and God forbid if you were ever on public assistance. What others thought of us was her main concern. That *always* mattered to my mom. Outside recognition was important to her, yet I wonder if she ever received that.

It was not so far-fetched, from what may be expected today. I grew up believing many things by watching my mom. She always taught me indirectly, unless it was cooking. Cooking, coloring, and playing cards are the only things my mom did hands on with me. While I was growing, some of the things I learned proved to be useless; other lessons I used as stepping stones, and those that remained, they molded me into becoming who I am today.

I tried constantly to get and meet my mom's approval while growing up. I strove to be a good girl, causing no problems for her. After all, I *could* see her daily struggles. I did not want to be an extra burden in anyway. I had stakes to set. I did not want to return to the Kay family; I wanted to be part of *my* family. I realized my mom never knew how afraid I was of being sent away permanently. I felt that at six years old and remained feeling the same discord until the age of forty. While writing this book, that realization truly made me sad! The positive thing is that we live and learn, and then we pass it on if we are aware!

> Trembling at men is a snare. But the one
> trusting in God will be protected.
>
> —Proverbs 29:25

CHAPTER 8

I was budding as a young girl, and entering fourth grade. I liked going to school, and my teacher, Mrs. Supple, was a good instructor. She was pregnant during that school year. I remember being on the swings with my newest friend Elizabeth. Mrs. Supple was with us, and I asked her if she was having a baby. You have to understand, back in the '70s, people did not ask any personal questions. At least, not in my family. Mrs. Supple was so kind. I do not recall much about that year. However, there was a new student, Elizabeth Allen, and as it turned out, she was God sent. She went on to be one of my deepest and truest friends, forty years later and counting.

Elizabeth came into our class after the September school year began. I watched her walk into the room with her uniform neatly pressed, and long blonde hair flowing down her back. I knew, as soon as I laid eyes on her, we were already friends forever. I, without any doubt, knew it! God again! I introduced myself to Elizabeth during lunch, and we became inseparable after that. We frequently walked hand-in-hand, skipping and singing and dreaming together. She and I spent nights at each other's homes, and suddenly, I felt less empty and more complete.

Fifth grade was memorable to me because my family had a new addition. My cousin Becca was born. The first and only girl cousin I was blessed with. I was so happy and excited. When meeting Becca for the first time, Auntie Rose refused to let me hold her. Fourth graders were babysitting. *Why couldn't I hold her?* Becca had the same tiny Polish nose that I had. I recall sitting on a plaid couch next to Auntie Rose, starring at Becca in all her perfect beauty. She was a baby angel in my mind. I loved her unconditionally from that day on.

That year, my teacher Ms. Florentine was a cross-eyed, very snub instructor. She always looked at us, out of the corner of her eye, while still looking forward. I know it sounds terrible; however, it is very truthful. Ms. Florentine proved to be very unkind, cold, and unforgiving. I was none of that though. I strove for others to like me simply because I had a likeable and kind personality. I went on to learn some hard but valuable lessons in reality regarding that very subject; the first being not everyone will like you, even if you are the most lovable person.

One spring day before walking to school, I went into our backyard and proceeded to pick a huge bouquet of lilacs for Ms. Florentine. They smelled so wonderful, and the color was a full bloom light purple. I loved the fragrance, and the color was extraordinary. Other than weeping willows, that was my favorite. Thinking it would delight my teacher and perhaps make her smile, I naively gave them to her. I smelled them all day, and the aroma took me away. Throughout the day though, the tape of Ms. Florentine accepting the flowers played repeatedly in my head. I kept recalling the expression on her face as unemotional. I had a pure heart giving those to her; however, she was unappreciative, and it hurt me immensely. As our day progressed in school, Ms. Florentine kept picking on me in a cruel manner. She called me out in front of the class repeatedly. I was so embarrassed, and I felt like she hated me but had no clue why. *Maybe*, I thought, *just maybe, she thinks I'm a brown-nose.*

When school was finished, I grabbed those lilacs from her vase. I looked Ms. Florentine square in her face as she stood by the door, escorting each student out. I knew she saw me take them from the corner of her eye. I threw my head back and walked down the hall. I was very proud of myself at that moment. Those fine lilacs went in a vase on my bedroom dresser. I felt no remorse for having taken them back. She, in my mind, did not deserve something so beautiful. Ms. Florentine had absolutely no reason to humiliate me, so I wanted to humiliate her back. She was very nice to me after that. Was it some sick joke on her part? I was confused. God went on to teach me that people are ugly, but it does not mean I have to be.

Elizabeth came to me at a time when I needed a girlfriend. I had to share all these horrible experiences I had gone through with someone who actually listened. The thing was, I never did it. I kept them hidden, air tight, with no exposure to the public. I knew Elizabeth had many responsibilities, and my life was not about to become one of them. Elizabeth's heart was pure and golden; she did not need to worry about me. In being friends with her, I learned about family illnesses of a different sort. I learned what a true and real down-to-earth girl she was, despite all she had endured.

I grew closer and closer to Elizabeth as the summer came and went. That September we had a nun, who in my opinion acted like the devil. We were in a Catholic school too. Sister Richter was our teacher. She was sinister, crude, and very military-like, calling us by our last names. Sister always seemed to humiliate the children who did not need it in their lives; and Elizabeth and I were two of them.

I could not believe it. Two years in a row with mean teachers. I was mentally beside myself with anguish. I just could not grasp their personalities. Being a teacher, I thought you were automatically nice. That was not true. Sister Richter was ten times worse than Ms. Florentine. I believed she must have been forced into teaching, because it was clear she did not want to be there.

The class assignment was to make Valentine's Day cards for our parents. I made mine for my mom and Steve, and was very proud of the job when it was completed. I was especially skilled at cutting hearts out from construction paper. Sister was walking the isles of the classroom, and I felt her peering over my shoulder, stopping abruptly at my desk. She glared down at the card, grabbing it. Sister Richter, proceeded to make me stand in the front of the class, explaining to the crowd who Steve was. I despised her after that. It was clear to me Sister knew exactly of my father's condition. That was a game Sister was playing in my mind, and I did not want to be engaged in it.

I became hardened to a degree. I still knew deep inside, I was a child of God, but my mind was becoming very hard. Sister made me callous. I was *always* singled out, and that meant more unnecessary pain to my young heart. Sister Richter always glared at her students, as if she looked down on them, as if we were beneath her. That was not Christ-like. I adamantly did not feel it should be that way.

One great morning, though, Father Vernon walked into our class. He proceeded to name off a handful of students to be excused. Sister was so livid when I was asked to go with him. I really loved Father Vernon. He was a great man who was devoted to the priesthood, Mickey Mouse, and

Disney. Father was putting on the production for the Annual Peach Festival, and I was to play Doc in the seven dwarfs. That small gesture of kindness proved to be a great distraction for me. I played the part for the next three years alongside of some of my best friends. In eighth grade, Elizabeth was chosen to play Snow White. During the next few years, while playing Doc, Father Vernon *booked* us at a few senior centers and VFW halls. That was a blast to be a part of. We had *gigs*, and everyone really enjoyed seeing the crowd smile. It was pure innocence, and pure joy.

I realized having and dealing with Sister Richter as a teacher was a test of my strength. She forced me to deal with situations and made me grow up quicker than I needed to. Looking back, it was not necessarily a bad thing, but for an eleven-year-old child, she made me deal with adult issues. I feel they were not things I should have had to confront as a sixth grader.

It was Fall when Steve drove my mom to buy our Sunday *Detroit Free Press*. I went for the ride. Two guys stood on the corner of 7 Mile and Van Dyke, selling the *Detroit News* and *Detroit Free Press*. My mom never bought *"The Detroit News"*. She told me "The *Free Press* is for the working people, the union folks; the *News* is for the rich." I found out, on my own, one leaned more toward the Republican view, and one the Democratic.

That particular Saturday evening, as we were picking up the paper, I was in the back seat of Steve's yellow Cadillac. I handed a letter to the paperboy, who looked to have been an upper teenager. The note stated that I thought he was cute, my name, and phone number. *Red flag!* When I handed him the letter, my mom asked what that was. As I told her, "a letter for the paperboy," Steve had already pulled off. I would say I knew it was not right, but I did not know the reason why it was wrong. My mom was angry; however, she never said another word. I did get an earful from Steve though. No, the paperboy never called. Thank God! Anything may have happened to me. Another moment of God's grace. Even though I never did believe anything bad would happen to me again, after my early childhood. That only proved how immature, dumb, and uninformed I was.

That act catapulted me to the onset of more boy-crazy behavior. I was a product of my upbringing and circumstances, without any realization of it. I did not know anything was wrong with my behavior, but I knew it would not be approved of. Josie was boy crazy, and she never got into trouble. I was curious, growing up in my early teens, but never did go past kissing a boy. I looked at them a lot and commented to Elizabeth. We daydreamed together.

Elizabeth and I had a sleepover during the summer, at her home. We sat on the porch, cat-calling some boys over. I ended up having my first French kiss with Freddie that evening, while we all played truth or dare. He did not want anything to do with me, other than to make it to whatever base he could. The kiss was as far as he got. I was going into seventh grade.

Even though I loved looking at and daydreaming about boys, I knew in my heart I would stay a virgin until I married. I felt it was the right thing to do. Why? That was not taught to me by my mom. But of course, we learned it in school and church. The only lesson my mom ever gave to my sisters and myself was to repeatedly say, "If you come home pregnant, I'll disown you." That is unloving and cruel to say to your child, when you, in fact, have never even had "the talk" with your daughter. That is something really horrible to say to a young girl who had been molested also.

The following summer, my mom took us to Boblo Island located in the middle of the Detroit River on the Canadian side. It was home to our local amusement park. We took a huge, double-decker party boat, which was docked behind Cobo Hall. It carried us under the Ambassador Bridge and down and around Windsor, Ontario. We had so much fun that summers day. It was a family event that included my grandparents, Auntie Nannette, and cousins. I have vague memories of the actual park itself, but I will never forget the boat ride.

Over the years, and on that particular day, my mom reminded us children how much she hated the water. She was afraid, never having learned to swim. Well, parents often relay their fears onto their children. That was the case with me. I, in my little mind, thought, *If mom is scared of water because she can't swim, I must be too*. And, so it goes! I never learned to swim, and I became deathly afraid of any bay of water along with bridges. I could tolerate being on land observing the water, but to be in it or on it took a lot out of me. It is factual that fears are created in one's mind. I do, most definitely, agree with that.

That same summer, though, I decided to venture out. Danny and I had mutual friends, who were brother and sister. Stella and Jimmy were very nice people to hang out with. They went to grade school with us. Stella was in my grade; Jimmy was in Danny's. Danny and Jimmy set up for a swim date at his home. Stella invited me, and I felt it a great opportunity to get familiar with water. Danny was so livid when I was invited. My mom drove both of us to 9 Mile and Ryan, and we stayed the day at their pool.

I waded in the shallow end because their built-in swimming pool went from three feet to fourteen feet. Yes, I was terrified. Danny laughed at me. "There was no reason to come if you can't swim." I disagreed and told him so. He was such a bully, always trying to intimidate me. Stella and I played in the water, and I pretended to swim. Jimmy called her to the deep end of the pool. I got out of the water and watched Stella dive and swim. She swam like a fish; I was so impressed. Danny convinced me to come into the deep end, saying he was going to hold onto me, that everything would be okay. I was too trusting. We were in the fourteen-foot section as he assured me, he would teach me to swim, and he would hold on tightly. I was so happy Danny was willing to do something nice for me. He never helped. The cold reality was he only took from me.

Danny let me go in that water and just swam away. I am convinced he tried to kill me. I was drowning. Jimmy jumped in, pulled me to the deck, and I began to gag and cry. It was at that point; I knew Danny did not want me around. But why? I had never done anything to him. I was only born. A predictable thing occurred upon returned home. You bet I told my mom. Her response played like a tape in my head for years to come. "Why are you always tattling? Can't you just keep your mouth shut?" was her comment. As an adult, I know what I would have liked to say back then. I would have calmly asked my mom what her reaction would have been had it been her it happened to. She was never there for me. I felt *all* alone.

> For God detests a devious person. But his close friendship is with the upright.
>
> —Proverbs 3:32

CHAPTER 9

For several years, after leaving the care of the Kay's, I still spent the summers in Port Austin with them. I did not realize it at the time, but my mom was paying Aunt Kate for my being there. I thought I was going to help her at the cottage because she and Uncle Ian loved me. In actuality, my mom hired her again for my care. Why did my mom think I was a baby? By then, I was going into seventh grade. I thought of myself as a young teenager, and I was growing very street smart. No one can teach you that in school. You learn it from growing up in the streets, as I did. I always had 75 percent full reign over what I did when with Aunt Kate.

My duties during that trip were not any different than when I was five years old. I was, however, no longer tide down to a curfew. I spent the entire day outside, about a mile from the cottage. I walked to the very tip of Michigan's thumb and basked in the hot sun with a spray bottle of water, for my skin. I proceeded to soak my hair in lemon juice, creating natural highlights. I shopped and browsed the stores, meeting new people. Aunt Kate's property was on Spring Street. I used to walk the same route as a kindergartner, and now I strolled it, nearing my teenaged years.

Under the bridge, on the way into town, there was a wonderful spill leading into Lake Huron. I never missed an opportunity to skip stones before passing by. Mona's boyfriend Dan taught me how to do that. "Pick the long flat rocks," he instructed. I got pretty skilled at skimming stones by the end of the summer. However, once I returned the following visit, I had to begin practicing all over again. It was a great time of exploring in my life. I liked being alone and having my fun, but I did miss Elizabeth. Being at Uncle Ian and Aunt Kate's was very enjoyable. It was a lifetime away from my born-into family's chaos. I learned lessons about life during that summer which remain with me today. Being up north felt logical and liberating; I longed to permanently stay there.

It was 1978 that year, and I ended up meeting an interesting guy while at the beach. He was traveling Lake Huron in his sailboat for the summer. Terry Holter was seventeen and originally from Pontiac, Michigan. I recall telling him I was fifteen. That summer became very memorable to me. I ventured out in search of independence with Kate Kay, while trying to stretch my wings as a young girl. I knew I had freedom with the Kay's. Freedom I did not have at home. Plus, I had no one with whom I had to share. I did my own things when I finished all my given chores.

For three days, Terry and I chatted, getting to know one another's personalities. I thought of myself as an interesting person, and I never had a problem communicating with adults. We talked a lot about music and our favorite bands. The topic of his travels came up, and he was headed to Florida from Port Austin. Terry was super attractive; with a great smile I can still picture till this day. He ended up asking me if I wanted to go for a ride on the sailboat the following day. Gosh, did I ever! But I had to get permission first. I walked back to the cottage and asked if I could go. See, in my mind I knew getting permission was the right thing. That was not, however, what a fifteen-year-old would do. She would have just gone.

Aunt Kate said no way. I tested her by saying I was going to go anyway. She was furious and threatened a whipping along with a call to my mom. Enough said! Yep, I was still being hit by my mom. I did walk back down to tell Terry I could not go. I believed, at the time, I was liked for my personality. Another very naive moment.

Terry and I hung out on the beach for the next week. We chatted and built sandcastles. It was all very innocent in my mind as we just communicated with each other. He never made an improper pass toward me, because I believe he surmised my actual age. He did, however, have a great ability, to talk about a variety of subjects. I wanted to stay in touch. We wrote letters after the summer was over. We continued corresponding for approximately three years afterward, although we never saw each other again.

I began realizing I did not like being told what I could and could not do. Aunt Kate was a thorn in my side, a cramp in my game. There honestly was no game to be had. Truth be told, I was just a daydreamer of a girl!

After meeting Terry, I soon came to see I was an older boy chaser. I wanted attention; and I never seemed to have the proper kind. All I longed for was a boy to love me, or even show interest in me. I figured it was what would bring me happiness. That started me on choosing the wrong kind of boys to attract.

Aunt Kate had a massive garage sale, and many neighbors dropped their items off for her to sell. There included an organ, clothes, and many pairs of platform shoes. I had never been to a garage sale, let alone aid in setting one up. Aunt Kate meticulously cleaned and organized all the goods. I recall many glassware and candles. I intently watched and learned, then I began helping. I was Aunt Kate's assistant in many ways, and I loved her as if she were my real aunt. At the end of Saturday, we cleaned the area and Aunt Kate counted the money. Upon finishing, she announced she was ten dollars short and accused me of stealing the cash. I had not done that, and my heart was broken. I was very uncomfortable and wanted to leave immediately after. I did not want to be around anyone who did not trust me. After all, I was a very good girl.

The remaining time at the cottage was short. I liked that idea. I was ready to start school and see Elizabeth, Joey, and Marie again. It is strange how things fall into place. Two weeks prior, I could not have fathomed wanting to go back to my born-into family. But now I just needed to get out of the environment I was in. I left that year feeling dirty and invalidated the moment Aunt Kate no longer trusted me. She was no longer any fun, and I did not return to her again until I was grown.

I had an inkling Aunt Kate spewed her thoughts of what I had done to my mom. Upon returning home, things were rougher and harder on me. My mom was standoffish and short-tempered with me. Gosh, I just got home from being gone for two-and-a-half months. No excitement for my return. I began to notice I continuously set myself up for failure with my family. If my mom was informed of what Aunt Kate thought, she never said a word about it to me.

As time went by, I missed Uncle Ian; however, I knew Aunt Kate had gotten to him first. My heart was torn apart. The last time I felt my heart ache like that was when I made my First Communion and was unable to see my dad. I was still thankful for all Aunt Kate taught me. She was a phenomenal woman, but she made a large error in judgment. I rationalized that in my head to make me feel better. I repeated it when I needed to.

My mind, as I learned, worked in a different manner than others. I got lost in my thoughts. I analyzed those thoughts, processing them in my own capacity, and many times, I let them go to God. After all, I did not know what to do and I had no one to turn to. I have absolutely no idea how I learned that technique. As I grew, I came to believe it was an internal mechanism, one that we are not all born with. I have to remind myself also, God is *my* savior. He has always been there for me, even when bad things occurred. I was faithful to Him and loved Him with all my heart. The church was my external escape from the chaos of my life.

> Keep on asking and it will be given to you; keep on seeking and you will find; keep on knocking and it will be open to you.
>
> —Matthew 7:7

CHAPTER 10

I often went to my grandparent's home on the weekends. I helped my grandpa collect paper from the neighbors, and then he and I took it to 12 Mile and Groesbeck Road to the recycle center. It was extra money for my retired grandpa, but moreover, it was productive time spent. He was a mover. Retired from Chrysler, my grandfather never sat still, unless John Wayne was on TV, or Grandma Katie called "lunch." He taught me to do the same, never allowing grass to grown under my feet.

I often earned my money from my grandparents. My grandma taught me how to clean a house from top to bottom, the Polish way. She was very structured but kind. Every other weekend, I took the removable cushions from the couch and chairs, and gave them a thorough vacuuming. Then I changed the bedsheets, dusted, washed windows, cleaned the bathroom, and scrubbed floors on my hands and knees. I never missed the chance to take a break to thumb through their *Readers Digest*. My job often included going down to the basement where it was very chilly, and I swept the painted gray cement floor. My grandma's instructions were very precise. I learned a great deal from her. She was a living angel to me.

For cleaning the entire home, my grandma would give me fifteen dollars. In the '70s and '80s, that was a lot and money to me. But on the way out the door or in the car, my grandpa always slipped me an extra ten to twenty dollars. He would lean into me and say, "You worked hard. This stays between the two of us." My grandpa always picked me up and drove me home when I went to clean. I loved our alone time. He was very intelligent and extremely knowledgeable. He purposely repeated the same stories from working and growing up. I heard them over and over again, until I listened, often asking questions. They truly are wonderful memories.

I'm so thankful for my loving grandparents. I believe many things in my life would have been even more tragic, if not for them. They both gave me stability and love, feelings I never received from my own family. My grandparents instilled responsibilities in me, teaching me what the joy of work really was. That is something that cannot be purchased. I often wondered, if perhaps my grandparents took me under their wings, because my mom never did. Quite possibly, they saw an opportunity to help me become a strong woman. My grandmother spent an enormous amount of time with me. Some of that time was me simply dropping by after school, walking two miles to their home. I never knew my grandma to turn me away, but instead she taught me, filled my belly with food, and made me laugh.

My grandma taught me to cook and clean, bake, can vegetables, and sew. She taught me about the love of God, and by possessing faith, it kept her going. She was an inspiration in many ways. Her iced tea was the best, and so were her get-togethers, homemade apple pies, and donuts. We lovingly referred to her donuts as "sinkers," because they were so heavy, but they were tasty. Each donut weighed about a quarter pound.

My Uncle Chris was a pivotal part of my life. I never gave much thought to the impact he had on me and my young mind. He was my mom's middle brother, and Uncle Chris had just come home from the Navy and Vietnam, in prior years. I recall being so happy to meet him. He gave us our photo and slideshow memories. Maybe he picked that up in the service, I do not know. He always had his slides going off for holidays and special occasions. I reminiscence about being a small child, going with my family to cut down Christmas trees up north. My grandpa was holding a handsaw in one hand, and was wearing his red lumberjack winter hat on the slide. That would only be a memory now, if not for Uncle Chris capturing it on film. He caught all the important moments on those photo slides.

Uncle Chris also took Danny and me to Belle Isle Park to fish one summers day. It was my first time ever going, and I remember the day vividly. Danny and I impatiently waited for my uncle to arrive that morning. I believe before Uncle Chris picked us up, we phoned him three or four times to be sure he had not forgotten. He drove us in his huge red Montego down East Grand Boulevard to Jefferson. He pulled alongside the curb, and we got our gear out. McDonald's was across the street from Belle Isle back then, and Uncle Chris treated Danny and me to lunch. I do not recall the fishing experience, but I do remember loving the day.

Uncle Chris's brother, my Uncle Joe, was also in the service representing the Marine Corp. Uncle Joe's wife was Auntie Rose, my cousin Becca's parents. They were lovely people, living a far distance from us. I saw them, and my cousins on special occasions only. I loved them very much and wrote frequently. They were encouraging to me because they seemed so happy together.

My mom's other sibling was my Auntie Nanette, and her husband, my Uncle Donald. Together, they eventually had three boys who were close to me growing up. Auntie Nanette was an excellent cook and baker. I loved her Polish *kapusta*, which is sauerkraut and fresh kielbasa. I think she traveled to Polish Market in Hamtramck and got the special mushrooms for the dish. Not those kinds of mushrooms! My mom and Auntie Nanette were amazing cooks, because my grandma taught them well. They were good for following recipes to the tee, but I liked to improvise. We had huge family gatherings for the holidays, and everyone brought something. The aroma was intoxicating.

I did, at the age of twelve, find out that my mom had another brother. Uncle Dave died at the age of eight, in 1956. I thought it very odd that he was never mentioned. We never saw his grave, and they never even acknowledged him. I, of course, because of my personality, asked my mom why they never talked about him. My mom explained how Uncle Dave and Auntie Nanette were walking on Van Dyke Road on a snowy day. A driver who was traveling the center lane never saw them crossing the street. He hit them both, killing Uncle Dave and injuring Auntie Nannette. My auntie was ten when that occurred. My mom commanded me to never talk about it to grandma. She said my grandma was still devastated, and she could not handle it. That had occurred at least twenty years earlier. I never discussed it with my grandma until many years later, as an adult. Uncle Dave apparently was in the hospital for a bit, before going to the light of God. My grandma had so much faith in God. She knew where Uncle Dave's soul was, but losing him forever changed her being.

I loved my aunts and uncles. They were warm individuals and upstanding people. Friday evenings were usually spent at Auntie Nanette's. My mom loaded Danny and me up in the station wagon, and we headed to Sterling Heights for the night. Occasionally, Henry would go too. On those Friday nights, my mom got her hair done by my auntie. I always enjoyed the opportunity to play with my cousins. Auntie Nanette was a hairdresser. She fixed my mom's hair while all of us kids listened to music, played Candyland, and watched *Planet of the Apes*. It was a time of play and growth with my cousins. They were not my first friends, like other families, and we only visited with them on Fridays and holidays.

My cousins and I always enjoyed one another's company. I remember always leaving after midnight. My aunt put my mom's hair up in her favorite hairstyle—a beehive. My auntie endlessly curled my mom's hair using tiny rollers, and continued with a stint under the hair dryer. My auntie then proceeded to "rat" my mom's hair into a coiffeur. On very rare occasions, Auntie Nanette cut my hair. Those were special times to me.

> Now we are giving you instructions, brothers, in the name of our Lord Jesus Christ, to withdraw from every brother who is walking disorderly and not according to the tradition that you received from us. For you yourselves know how you should imitate us, because we did not behave in a disorderly way among you.
>
> —2 Thessalonians 3:6–7

CHAPTER 11

In seventh grade, I began showing signs of a troubled girl. I liked being a clown, but at the same time had a very loving and giving disposition. Sometimes in Mr. Borski's class, I acted out or talked while he was teaching. It was enough of a disturbance to him one day, and I was dismissed from his class, having been sent down to the teacher's lounge. There, I saw a well-dressed male social worker. I do not have any recollection of the person, but I do recall the conversation.

He asked several questions about my home life, being extremely covert as to when he brought up my father. He inquired about my extended family, including my grandparents, aunts, uncles, cousins, and so on. I was perplexed but answered all of his questions. I had manners and respect. I was taught that. Moreover, I was smart not to give too much information out. That would definitely upset my mom. She was quick to always tell us, "What goes on in this house stays in this house." Yes. I guess it did. That night, while we all ate dinner, I told my mom what happened. She was enraged, grilling me on what I was doing in class, that got me sent down to a social worker. I was so sad. I was not doing anything more than my male classmates. I thought I was being funny and fitting in. Nothing was ever mentioned after that.

After that instance, in my eyes, I thought my mom would treat me differently. However, she continued to cuddle to me and tell me she loved me a bushel and a peck. Did I believe it? Absolutely! Why would I not? She was my mom. Did I think my household was normal? Yes! Putting aside the fact that my dad was ill and I had been abused, we had a good life. My mom was providing for all of us. We had food on the table, clothes on our backs, and all six of us attended a Catholic school. I had awesome grandparents from my mom's side, terrific aunts and uncles and Elizabeth.

My mom degraded me a lot. She said things like "Why do you talk so much? I'm going to buy you a muzzle for Christmas," or "I'll give you a nickel if you can keep your mouth shut until we get home." Today I know, as a child, thinking everything was normal is what saved me. If I had believed something was wrong with *me*, I could not be who I am today. Ordinary is not what I encountered or endured. I am not blind. I must say, my household was highly dysfunctional. I also want to add that there is no such thing as "normal." That term is used so freely, as if it is something to live up to. I am here to tell you, normal does not exist. Normal is a state of existence in the mind, but absent in reality!

In the summer, before the beginning eighth grade, a tragic event unfolded in the neighborhood. A local acquaintance, Brandy, was found lying in the alley, kitty-cornered from my house. Brandy lived on Mound, behind Bernie's Bar. Why was she walking in the alley at that time of night? I distinctively remember, sitting on the oversized chair, watching the Donnie and Marie Variety Hour. Steve came bolting through the front door from the neighbor's home to find me in front of the television. He was frantic, coming inside to check on me. Where was my mom? That was her job! She was still at the neighbor's house. Steve explained very briefly what had taken place.

The police cars surrounded the street as the officers rushed to the alley, finding Brandy. She was covered in blood, beaten, and raped with a stick. She was two years younger than me. The young man responsible was caught shortly afterward. I felt so badly for Brandy and had no words to console her with. While the suspect was sitting in the back of the police cruiser, I pointed to the window and said, "God will punish you." Steve quickly directed me into the house, scolding me. One thing I will say about myself is that very little scared me. After that happened to Brandy, I was more cautious though, and never walked the alleys again.

Following that incident, Marie's mom and dad paid for Brandy to go to the same Lutheran school on Outer Drive and Mound that Marie attended. Marie's parents felt they wanted to do something, to help the family out, but that only lasted a couple of semesters. The parochial school had too many rules for Brandy. During that time, Marie, her parents, and I started a karate class at the YMCA in downtown. Yes, the same one my dad lived in. It was a waste of money for my mom because I never took it seriously. My mom made comments to me saying, "All you have to do is start talking and they'll let you go." *What the hell did that mean?* When she constantly put me down and belittled me, I began feeling worse about being me.

Grade school was coming to an end. Eighth grade was so fun, but challenging for me. Our teacher was an outstanding person. Sister Gaudlia was dynamic, charismatic, and funny. Oh, how Elizabeth and I both clung to her, loving Sister with every ounce of our beings. She was a tough, loving teacher who taught us about empathy, compassion, and not judging a nun by her habit. Sister Gaudlia, who, for the first time in all my life of being taught by a nun, did the unthinkable. She lifted her habit up in the back and exposed her short silver-gray hair to the whole class. There were gasps and chuckles. Doing something like that was unheard of. Nuns were sisters to look up to and admire. They never showed us a human side, until now.

Sister was so terrific a lady, looking back. She taught us to accept, have tolerance, and love each other, as God does us. In the spring of 1980, Sister convinced the others in the convent and Monsignor to allow the nuns to get a puppy. They picked a golden retriever. He was invited into our class several times. That lady was an amazing trailblazer. Sister taught practicality and laughter in her classroom. Today, I pray she is working alongside God, assisting Him in doing great things for our futures, and in His light.

Elizabeth taught me about victory and defeat when we both tried out for the school cheerleading squad. I watched as after the competition, she threw her huge circled number in the toilet, flushing it. That circle contained a number that signified the order in which we competed for a spot on the team. I remember exactly what I said to Elizabeth that night, as my mom drove us in her station wagon. "I only got chosen because I have a big mouth." I hoped, at the time, it made her feel better. What I later realized, when I grew older, was that the negative things spoken to me, about me, had taken root inside my head.

Elizabeth's mom was ill while we were growing up. I never knew her diagnosis, but for a couple years, Mrs. Allen was in a wheelchair. Very thin and frail, she was unable to do many mom functions. Elizabeth and I frequently spent the night at each other's homes on weekends. Danny tried his skills of manipulation on her too. I warned Elizabeth immediately and told her to stay away from him. Elizabeth was the firstborn of three girls. Her responsibilities were very different than mine. She was the oldest; I was the baby of my family. Her duties included taking care of her sisters in a household way; however, I found out later on that Elizabeth did much more.

It seems sexual abuse happened quite a bit in the '60s and '70s, just like mental illness, but was never discussed. Many of us suffered as a result. I was lucky, I thought, because the abuse only took a small toll on me thus far. Many girls were confiding in each other. Not me though. Elizabeth was not talking either. Our graduation from eighth grade was not memorable, but listening to Alice Cooper belt out "School's out for summer, school's out for ever…" was my highlight. Elizabeth was facing huge challenges with her mom at home. We never discussed a thing, so I had no clue.

The summer was filled with many changes as Joey, Marie, and I separated from each other. They were doing much more together, and I was an outsider because my priorities were getting ready for high school and Elizabeth. Joey and Marie were kids to me. Elizabeth and I did all types of things together, from delivering flyers for her mom, to shopping at Eastland Mall. We cooked at her home together, indulging in eating raw beef. Back then it was safe, not like today, and we piled on the salt and ate it. Elizabeth and I had many common interests too. She made it easy to love her.

My oldest brother, John, and his longtime girlfriend, Lynn, got married in Florida. My mom did not go. She had to work and chose not to take the time off. The pictures were very nice, and John was so handsome that day. Both John and Lynn moved to Chicago, as Lynn was in college. They went to be with Lynn's parents in Florida for a vacation, and they ended up getting married. John was nineteen, and Lynn was eighteen. I will admit, when John left our home in Detroit, it killed my soul. He was all I had at the house. I do not know how I ever overcame him leaving.

> When under trial, let no one say, "I am being tried by God." For with evil things, God cannot be tried, nor does he himself try anyone.
>
> —James 1:1

CHAPTER 12

High school consisted of four memorable years at another Catholic community. I officially dropped the family title of Barbara and went by Barb. The only people who ever acknowledged the name change were my grandparents and Auntie Nannette and Uncle Don I needed to be who I was, whomever that was, and my name was the beginning. All of my teachers referred to me as Barb. How refreshing that was. High school was different than grade school. My personality was not embraced by any popular girls. I was very popular at St. Louis the King. That time of change was scary to me.

I tried out for the freshman cheerleading squad, and to my surprise, I made the team. There were many girls who were really great with the splits. Although I did do mine during tryouts, it was by God's grace. Tryouts were fun and not as intimidating as I expected. They went smoothly. It was a time of White Rain hair spray, white tennis shoes, and competitions. I was meeting and making new friends. High school was not grade school. It was the big time, and during freshman year, I loved it. We had Candygrams and Shamrocks we were able to buy, and then have them delivered to whomever we liked. We passed great notes during class, and they never make it to the teacher's desk. We made pom-poms for the floats, had multiple friend sleepovers, and went to the local carnivals in the Fall.

Danny was attending the same school when I arrived. He had already been there for a year, but that was all about to change. He was still a very angry person. I never found out the specifics, because I was told it did not concern me. However, sophomore year, Danny took a swing at the dean of students. He was expelled immediately. I was so happy to see him go. I did not like seeing him in or out of school. After he left, my remaining time was extremely enjoyable. People who thought I may act in the same manner quickly got to see I was not Danny in any way.

In 1980, there was still a course being taught for home economics at my high school. In that class, I met some seniors who constantly teased me. Mrs. Anne Prunke was our teacher. She went on to show me how to sew on a machine (just like Mona and Aunt Kate), how to cut lettuce without using a knife, and how to prepare a meal, having it simultaneously finish. Those were extremely important things to learn. I took pride in the class, and I was learning new techniques for cooking and sewing.

Here, I additionally learned from the upperclassmen. They were seniors, taking the class, simply because they needed another credit in order to graduate. They cared less about the class, and were clowns and set out to prove it. I learned sexual terminology during the year also. I was made fun of by Brian and Martin for not knowing what certain words meant. I did find out the answers when I got home one night. Leslie was washing the dishes, and I pointblank asked her. She whipped her whole body around to answer the questions. First, I was berated, then she told me what everything was. Oh! The next day, Brian and Martin got an earful. They made fun of me for being a virgin, but deep inside, I think they were intrigued.

They did crazy things to Mrs. Prunke, like taking a banana from her drawer and putting it into the washing machine. The next hour, they would buy another from the store, returning it to her drawer. She looked all over for that banana. On another day, they ran fishing line over the lights at the ceiling and tied a Pillsbury Doughboy to the other end. During class, while our teacher taught, they began to lower it down into her face. Then, just as she reached for it, they pulled it back up. I was shocked at how brazen they were, but truth be told, it was hilarious. I think Mrs. Prunke was very tolerant toward these boys because they were seniors, and it was in fun.

I was not a studious individual. Although I enjoyed school, it was the socializing that attracted me. I loved chatting with teachers and new acquaintances; it is what fulfilled me. I asked them questions about life, and they always made time for me. I met another girl in freshman year, Whitney Singer, during gym class. I absolutely hated that course; it was by far the hardest I had to take. I was not inclined to "working out," running, or jogging. In my young mind, those were the exercises that one gradually learned to do.

Ms. Marine forced us into running laps around the football field. I was not happy! Whitney and I would take our time, going at one another's pace. I was not able to jog easily, so Ms. Marine made it a point to call me out all the time. It was Sister Richter and sixth grade all over again. I started to regress. I began to go from having fun to feeling like I was being ganged up on again. I refused to be too involved with anything having to do with gym class. If she had just taken some time to be a good teacher, I may be healthier today. I say that with truth, not sarcasm.

There is much fact in the comment that one person can make a difference. Unfortunately, like anything, there is a positive and negative effect that can be had. It all depends on who is doing the teaching, demonstrating, or talking. I have, over the years, learned how to filter and differentiate what needs to go into my mind and memory. However, as a fourteen-year-old, it was added strain on me.

I felt different in high school because I did not know any other students. I, over time, did of course make friends. Those people, though, were not privy to knowing about my dad or my past. I had tons of acquaintances because of my personality; by tenth grade, people knew and understood my sense of humor, and most appreciated my ability to talk. I loved English and Math, and I began excelling in those classes.

Cheerleading, pep rallies, football games, and hanging with my friends was my life. I enjoyed being on the Crusaders cheer team. My fondest memory is a cheer competition we had at the Pontiac Silverdome. It is the same stadium where the Detroit Lions played at that time. I was on the field, smack dab in the center of the helmet. How luck and blessed I felt to have that moment. God was again working on my behalf.

In the two years I was a cheerleader, my mom never once came to a single game to watch me. Not even at the Silverdome. Her excuse was "I have to work" or her famous line: "I'm really too busy, Barbara." Why, then, did my mom go to Danny's basketball or football games, and not mine? The obvious is that she did not care about me. Yes, she cared for me; however, it was purely out of obligation.

I was often referred to as "moody" by my mom, and I was. I did not know where I fit in, or if I even did. I had a handful of close friends, but only three true comrades. Elizabeth, who was living in Metamora, Michigan, now; Whitney; and a new friend, Charmaine. Whitney, Charmaine, and I hung out exclusively, in and out of school. We had sleepovers at each other's homes, or hopped on a bus, going to Lakeside Mall to buy stickers at the store. We hung out, playing and listening to Journey and Loverboy. I miss those days in many ways. They were filled with innocence, pure fun, and very few responsibilities.

My mom was pretty much absent from my teenaged days. She worked days, and weekends were spent with Steve over at his place. The only people left in the house were Leslie, Henry, Danny, and myself. Josie and John had moved out. Leslie and I kept the house immaculate, so there was very little to do but have fun. I did not have anyone telling me not to do something. My mom left us in charge of ourselves for three years. If I needed something, I asked for it, usually getting it.

At the time, Henry went on dates and needed to impress the ladies. He recruited me to iron his shirts and jeans before he went out. I loved doing the job for him. I charged him, but I only got paid a handful of times. I felt great about myself, having made Henry look good. When he left for the night, he had fresh-pressed creases in his jeans, his shirt was pristine and he looked so handsome.

There was no working job in my life, other than babysitting on occasion or cleaning for my grandma. I was not employed, though, at a job taking out taxes. I had many odd jobs growing up. I sold flowers under the vidox on 8 Mile and I-75 when I was nine, cleaned the church on occasion, and cleaned the local beauty parlor. When I asked my mom to take me clothes shopping, she handed me her Hudson's charge card, telling me to go shopping at Eastland Mall. I walked a half mile, catching the 8 Mile bus, and off to the mall I went. Knowing my mom did not have a lot of money, I never took advantage of her. I bought what I needed, spending under sixty dollars for one pair of pants, and two skirts. I loved Gloria Vanderbilt pants but could never afford them. The price back then was fifty dollars a pair. I was never frivolous with the charge card. Truth be told, I was always appreciative. My mom still sent disapproving looks, once I showed her what I thought were great finds. I said *why* to myself many times. I never understood what I was doing wrong in her eyes.

I liked many of my teachers throughout high school. We were privy to many advantages that did not occur in a public school. We learned meditation in religion class when our teacher, Mrs. Lappin, instructed us on other types of learning and other religious beliefs. I was fascinated by those teachings. I was enthralled and taken in, and my mind was absorbent, like a sponge. Mrs. Lappin took me to many different places through meditation. It was so enlightening!

While in school, we did on occasion have a motivational speaker come in to talk with us. In Mr. McCloony's government class, we had a gentleman by the name of David Toma, speak one afternoon. He was engaging, and captured my attention. Mr. Toma spoke with passion and conviction. That really caught my attention. I thought, *I'd really like to do this someday in a format regarding my dad's illness*. Well, that was not a fleeting thought. I knew instinctively I had the ability do it; I was a great talker when it was a subject I liked. I did not have a clue on how that would ever come to be though.

High school, once I began to really make friends, was very fun. That is the entire point. It was fun. My mom had already imbedded the seed in my head that I was not going to college, unless I worked or got a grant. I babysat; that was far from affording college. I never applied myself because no one prepared me for something greater. There was no need to excel. For what? I was always told I would work a labor job. I had to allow that to sink in. My mother never thought I could excel at anything. Why though?

In tenth grade, I got "the talk" from Leslie, my middle sister. Sad, I felt. I envisioned it, coming from my mom, over breakfast together. I was so naive when it came to communication. I did not see that my thoughts of how I expected things should be and the way things really were, amounted to two different realities. I always tried to get validation from my mom; however, it never came to pass. Not even as an adult. By the time Leslie talked to me, I had made it to nearly third base. Why did they wait so long to approach me?

In tenth grade, I thought you could possibly become pregnant by dry-humping with a boy. Leslie did not get explanatory; she just told me about foreplay. Important things were never explained to me. But why not? Was it because of what happened with James when I was in first grade? My mom, nor anyone else, knew about what Danny had done to me. It was puzzling then, and I still cannot figure that out. My mom, in my eyes, loved me. She said she did. I always thought her behavior meant love! I always thought her behavior meant love? Yes. I knew nothing else, no other way. I did, unexpectedly, get a small talk from Steve. The extent of what he tried to relay was that all boys are only looking for sex. Steve went on to say he was once young, and he knew from experience.

In sophomore year, my sister Josie got married in Tennessee. It was the first of three. I got to stand up in the wedding as a bridesmaid. I had never been to a wedding, let alone walk down the aisle for one. The excitement was overwhelming, and I loved it. There was a hustle and bustle in Josie's house, getting the preparations underway. The church service itself was nice, but the weekend afterward was another horrible time because of my mom.

I felt great during that trip. I remember it vividly. Ms. Karen, my mom's friend, and her daughter, Susan, came with us to Knoxville for the wedding. Susan and I were occasional friends when we visited each other. We had many sleepovers together in the past, but she and I were not close. When we spent time alone, we did have fun.

After the wedding reception at the church, everyone went back to Bob and Josie's home, for the after-party. There were not many people our age, so Susan and I ventured out. There were railroad tracks at the back of Josie's property line. Susan was an observant girl when it came to boys. She had bragged to me about "putting on a raincoat for a guy" when I was in seventh grade. It took me days to realize what she was talking about. Susan was fast, much faster than I!

Susan said she saw some boys hanging out by a house, down on Merchant Road, just before the Railroad tracks. I was fifteen; she was fourteen. I remember walking by the house several times with her. When the boys noticed us, we ended up going onto the porch, eventually going inside and drinking beer. These were strangers neither of us had ever met. *Red flag!*

I can tell you exactly what I was thinking. I thought Susan and I would just have a bit of fun, flirt, and then head back to my sister's party. I was such a simpleton. I really had no experience with boys, especially boys who appeared to be in their twenties. Susan and I engaged in small talk when we walked into the house. The guy I was chatting with said his name was

John Adams. I instantly doubted that but continued flirting. He was slick. He gave me a story about having just gotten out of the Army, he "wanted to get lucky." I was not falling for it; however, I did not know what boundaries were. I was never taught that, and the people who invaded my comfort zone never had consequences. I did stay, and took it too far. I allowed the guy to kiss me, touch my breasts, and dry-hump me. My clothes never came off. I would not have done that. I guess you could say, perhaps guys thought I was a tease. I thought I was only having fun and I was merely stretching my horizons.

Apparently, Susan and I were gone for a long time and did not realize it. The troops came marching in, literally. As we saw people from my sister's property on foot with flashlights, we also witnessed cars driving up and down Merchant Road. People were calling out our names. Oh, my gosh! Busted! I called out for Susan to hurry up and come out of the back room. There were many folks on the porch, just hanging out, chatting, and drinking beer. They also warned us that people were fast approaching.

I grabbed Susan by the arm, and we made a beeline to the gas station on the corner. The entire time, I was frantic about getting into trouble. Susan cared less. She never knew punishment like I did. I knew what was coming for me. I kept going over possible scenarios for what my mom would do to me as Susan and I walked down the road. We pretended we were walking back from the gas station. My mom was beyond pissed, even once she saw us coming toward her. My brother John was frantic. He grabbed my hand, holding it, and walked with me back to the house. He leaned into me and said, "Don't ever do that crap again." I knew he loved me at that moment and reassured him that I would not.

Ms. Karen did absolutely nothing to Susan, and that enraged my mom. Yes, enraged! Susan and I were sleeping in the basement for the weekend, and there we were sent upon getting back to Josie's house. Once our pajamas were on, my mom and Ms. Karen came down. My mom began to verbally insult me, and then she struck me several times, beating me like a dog. I could not believe it. At sixteen, I was getting hit by her. I was, once again, humiliated because of my mom. She was in the game of using me for setting examples. I never figured that one out either. I cried that night as Susan comforted me. She later told me, "I got laid." Great, she got lucky; and I got in trouble for it. I knew I should never have stayed at that strange house. I did not want to leave Susan in the beginning, but after drinking a few beers, I chose not to leave at all.

The trip home from Tennessee was filled with more insulting behavior from my mom. Did she not know I had gotten it the first time? She was beating an injured person, and my mom was skilled at doing that. I believe my mother did those things to look impressive to Ms. Karen. You know, she wanted to be the disciplinary. Well she was, but is that what real love looks like? Of course not! Weeks after coming home, my mom admitted she wanted to teach Mrs. Karen an example of good parenting skills. That was so ridiculous to me. Good parenting skills? That became my ongoing joke to myself.

The following year in June, Josie and her husband Bob welcomed into the world a perfect baby girl. Her name was Brenda; I was taken in, to the point of elation. I met Brenda that July and immediately fell in love with her.

> Now the works of the flesh are plainly seen and they are sexually immoral, uncleanness, brazen conduct, idolatry, Spiritism, hostility, strife, jealousy, fits of anger, dissensions, sects...and things like these... those who practice such things will not inherit God's kingdom.
> —Galatians 5:19–21

CHAPTER 13

I longed for a date in high school, but my mom did not allow it. I never understood that either. I was a cute girl, with what I considered a great personality. But boys at that age are not at all interested in how nice you are. They are quite honestly concerned with sex and making a homerun. I had already heard a bit from Leslie and Steve. I had an idea of what was going on.

In eleventh grade, a senior named Greg asked me to the homecoming dance. We had a good time and did go out on a few dates, never hitting it off. Even though I was molested as a young girl, I was a virgin in my mind. I never asked, agreed to, or invited those things to happen to me, so I was still a virgin. I felt that played a huge part in not having dates in high school. I had the radar going on.

Eleventh grade was memorable for me. I was in the backgammon and science clubs. Mr. Conley was the facilitator of the backgammon club. Josie had originally introduced me to the game. I really enjoyed playing, but was never in competition with anyone. That is not how the game is played. I learned competition is healthy and welcomed when playing sports or board games. My fellow classmate and friend always played with me. Jerome taught me what competition was all about.

I learned how to play for fun and how to play to win. After classes on a given day, the club members met in the school library. There, Mr. Conley set all the boards up, and the students took to their tables. Jerome and I always played against each other. We were already friends in school, so being in the club brought us closer together. During that time, I became better and more competitive as a player. Competition never appealed to me in any way.

Jerome's dad, Officer Chesapeake, was a Detroit police officer. He, one spring evening, snuck the two of us into Cobo Hall for the Culture Club concert. What excitement. Jerome and I had a blast, but I was overly concerned about Officer Chesapeake getting into trouble, because we did not have tickets. Everything went off without a hitch though, and Jerome and I had a bonding moment as friends. I came to learn, getting into concerts was a perk of an officer's job.

The high school I attended had quality instructors. I never had the opportunity to tell my favorite teacher, Mrs. Susan McMullan, how much she meant to me. She taught me history and yearbook. Mrs. McMullan was another one of those adults in my life whom I will never forget. She was the type who was hip and stylish. Mrs. McMullan smiled a lot and had a very outgoing, fun personality. She helped mold me into a lady simply by watching her mannerisms. Always right on point, she never took gruff from her students. I liked that. No sass in her class! In senior year, we had our yearbook party at her home. It was a twenty-five-minute drive for my mom, and it seemed like such a long distance to me. What an amazing time we had, and she kept a gorgeous home. It was a time of *Thriller*, and Michael Jackson was hot, so it was fitting the party featured his album. I remember the smell of pine and cinnamon in her home. It was so warm and comfortable.

Another wonderful woman and teacher was Mrs. Claudia Onefer. She was sharp as a pin, both on outside appearances, and when it came to teaching English. Mrs. Onefer pushed me to excel at writing and poetry. English was, by far, my favorite class. She and Mr. Clothe, my freshman English teacher, were instrumental in helping me become a reader and writer. I indulged in writing additional poetry in high school, and even continued writing after graduation. It became a surprise to me, because according to my mom, I was just going to work a labor job. Poetry was really unheard of. It was something my mom certainly did not *get*. I went on to have my poems displayed on Mrs. Onefer's bulletin board. I was overjoyed when one of my poems made it into the senior yearbook.

The arts appealed to me a great deal. Going downtown to the Detroit Institute of Arts, viewing the building's architecture, and E. E. Cummings were my favorite pastimes. I often daydreamed about professions I was interested in, only if I were smart enough: psychologist, teacher, or journalist. I was clear I wanted an occupation helping others. I wanted a career where I worked hands-on, helping others. My thoughts are these: If you know in your heart what you long to do on a professional level, it is up to you to fulfill that goal. Do not wait for others help; be strong and determined. Every one of us has a talent. Nurture it, and watch it bloom. You only have to be good at one thing; just do it better than anyone else can.

A tragic event took place senior year for me. My dear friend from grade school, Paul Holbrook, called me to tell me the news. The doctors found a tumor in his brain. Apparently, he had it since he was a child, but no one knew. Paul explained to me during that phone call he was going into the hospital for surgery. I prayed so very hard for him. He was the straight A student all through school, and I had gone from first through eighth grades with him.

Paul attended school at Sacred Heart Seminary, but another school he was affiliated with was having a basketball game. I was invited and never went. Paul's older brother, Edward, who went to school with my brother, Henry, came to pick me up. Not only was I not ready; I could not go. I had been so melancholy for hours, and I had no strength to gather myself up. Edward was completely angry, saying I should have at least called him. But Ed did not understand that I was unable. I felt a total sadness wash over me; however, I could not pinpoint why. I believed it was the teenaged years and hormones at the time. I later talked with Paul, explaining the truth about feeling melancholy. In my head, I thought I was starting my cycle for the month; I was always moody then. Paul understood, but I could tell in his voice he was disappointed I had not attended the game. Little did I know, I was showing signs of mental illness in my mood swings.

During my final year at St. Clement, a friend of mine introduced me to *Leatherneck* magazine. It was a military publication for the enlisted population. I instantly began compiling letters that evening to the gentlemen who were in the pen pal section of the magazine. I wrote four letters that night and received a response from every one of the soldiers. I continued to write them all for several years, adding many names to my *friends*.

Christmas of 1983, I invited a marine to my home for me to host. Dave and I had become very close friends over a period of time. We shared poems, pictures, and gifts with one another. He was so handsome and strong. That is what truly appealed to me. Dave was the sincere type who fell for *me*, hard. We ventured out to Oakland Mall while he visited. Dave asked me to sit on a bench and wait for him to come back. I was skeptical, afraid he would leave me at the mall. In actuality, Dave was buying me a promise ring. Excitement poured out of me immediately, then I was scared. Scared at what the ring meant, but I excepted it.

Once in Detroit a few days, Dave bought a ticket for me to fly back to Pennsylvania with him. He wanted me to meet his family. Whew! That was too much for me, and my body shut down, making me very sick. I could not go. Dave was so disappointed, and I understood why. I felt for him, I did. However, I was not ready for that type of a relationship obviously, because I got ill. Dave was nineteen, getting ready to turn twenty in June. I had just turned seventeen. We continued to write, but things were never the same. The chemistry was no longer there.

The same year, while on a walk through the neighborhood, I met a young man. Matthew was nineteen and lived on his own. We quickly struck up a conversation, and over time became close. His studio apartment was so tiny but quaint. The building sat across the street from my secret hideout. We spent many days at his place, chatting and making plans to be together. I always thought I would wait until I was married, but there was an undeniable sexual bond between the two of us. Matthew and I made out and fondled each other. He once gave me two hickeys on each of my cheeks. I was very taken in by him. He was good-looking, kind, and had an amazing personality. He treated me like an adult, and spoke to me as an equal. I had not experienced that since meeting Terry back in Port Austin. When my mom questioned the hickeys, I told her they were pinch marks from Grandma B on the corner. If she did not believe me, she never said a word. I am very relieved to report Matthew and I never did get to home base. I was too afraid and told him so. He was a gentleman about it, but I never saw him again.

I considered myself to be boy-crazy. I liked the attention I got. I never received that kind of *love* from my family. I stayed true to myself and was not sexually active though. I considered myself to be a good Catholic girl, but in actuality, I was not. I often thought of doing something, then wonder *what would God say to me, what would grandma and grandpa say?* That made me question my actions a bit longer.

At the time, I was trying to sell space for the yearbook ads at school. Being on the yearbook committee, I took my job seriously. I scoured my immediate neighborhood and went to all my favorite visiting spots, selling space. Mr. Frank, from the dry cleaners, bought a quarter page ad. I loved him for supporting me. He was a great old soul.

I ventured into a new chiropractor office, where Lynn's dad had his business years prior. It was across the street from my grade school and next door to the salon I used to clean as a young girl. Upon walking into the office, I met Dr. Hal Gonzales and Dr. Sam Stork. Dr. Gonzales bought an ad, and Dr. Stork hired me to babysit. It was a great day. Dr. Gonzales offered me an adjustment and x-rays after our meeting. I had been familiar with getting adjustments, because Lynn practiced on me. I agreed, never informing my mom. *What would she care?* I thought.

I loved babysitting for Dr. Stork. His wife, Sing, had a sweet and beautiful disposition. Their two daughters were loving and happy babies. On occasion, when I was babysitting, Dr. Gonzales who lived next door came to visit me. We laughed a lot, and he watched me do my homework on the patio table.

I was seventeen, Hal was twenty-seven when we began an intimate relationship with each other. He invited me over to watch television, but we ended up chatting for hours. On one occasion, while there, Hal sat me on his lap and began kissing and fondling me. It was my first encounter with an older man. He began taking it to home base, but I could not. Today, as an adult, I wish the timing was better. I wanted to be with him, and I believe it could have been a great growing experience. However, everything in divine order.

Hal also introduce me to the college life. He drove me to Bowling Green University, showing me around the beautiful campus. Their buildings were gorgeously designed, and the inside of the classrooms were jam-packed with books. I longed to be in college, so I applied but was denied. At least, for a moment in time, someone believed in me. Dr. Gonzales and Dr. Stork eventually dissolved their partnership. Dr. Gonzales moved to Ohio, and Dr. Stork moved up north. I never saw either doctor again.

In May of 1984, I graduated from high school. Out of 115 students, I was close to the bottom for grade point average. My C average was good enough to graduate but hardly enough for the real world. I knew college was not an option because of my mom, and the fact BGU denied my admission. I was not smart enough to get a grant or scholarship for college, and knew without it, I was not going to attend another school. Truth be told, I did not think there was anything I was good at, except talking. Out of the six of us children, Josie was the only one who went to college. The rest of us were doomed for menial work.

> Whoever trusts his own heart is stupid but the
> one who walks in wisdom will escape.
>
> —Proverbs 28:26

CHAPTER 14

All the experiences I had with boys and men, and Mom never knew it. Once she had Steve in her life, her children became a second priority. Do not get me wrong; I loved my alone time, but I longed for a mom. I longed to be her priority. Two weeks after graduation, I loaded up a small trailer onto the back of my Nova SS and moved to Knoxville, Tennessee. My sister Josie still lived there with her family. I moved into the mother-in-law apartment that connected to their home. It was a small space. There was a room which the bed was in, a kitchen, and a bathroom. I had my own entrance too.

Even though it was a tiny space, it fit everything I owned. The bed and kitchen set belonged to Bob and Josie. They let me borrow them. Everything else was mine. The time spent with Brenda was amazing and wonderful. She was such a happy baby, and I frequently watched her. She and I sang and play constantly. I loved that little girl so much. I knew for sure, someday, I wanted children. That was the extent of the thought.

Staying under someone else's roof, even when you are paying rent, does not always work out. Josie was demanding of me. Because I was right there, she considered me to be the built-in babysitter. I did not mind that arrangement in the beginning, but I was nearing eighteen, and I longed for a life of my own. I was watching Brenda every weekend and after work some days. Bob and Josie went to exercise at the gym when they got done working. Many days, they left it to me to pick up Brenda from daycare. As time went on, though, it became apparent I was being taken advantage of. In my mind, though, family was supposed to help, so I did. It was me once again not having healthy boundaries.

ABANDONED WITH FAMILY BUT NEVER BY GOD

I got a phone call from my mom one Sunday morning. She was calling to tell me my good buddy, Paul Holbrook, had died. He had his brain surgery but did not recover. I was so hurt and saddened with guilt. I wished I had gone to that damn basketball game with him. I wanted to get back to Detroit for the funeral, but not one person would lend me the money. Not John, Josie, or my mom. I missed Paul's funeral. It took me some twenty years to get over that.

At the time of watching Brenda, I was not even aware that boundaries were needed. I simply was never taught that. All those times my mom had teaching moments with me, and she never even said a word unless negative. I was getting fed up with being in the predicament with Bob and Josie, so I decided to do something about it. Boundaries show self-love and strength. They are healthy to have. It took a long time for me to really register that thought in my head, finally loving myself enough to do it.

I was working two jobs at the time, and did not like that my free time was not my own. After four months of staying with my sister and her family, I moved out. I got my very own apartment, but still within walking distance of Brenda and my jobs. I no longer had a vehicle, so I walked wherever I needed to go. My main job was working as a waitress for Shoney's Restaurant. I walked twenty-five-minutes each way, every day, in a dress and pantyhose. No matter what the weather was, rain, heat, or snow, I did what I had to do to get to work. There was no one to take me, although I wish there had been.

I was taught to be a hard worker. I was committed to doing a great job in whatever I touched. I went out of my way for my employers and customers to prove that. I really liked working in the restaurant. I enjoyed the quick pace and the ever-changing crowd. I became friends with many coworkers, including my first love, Ben. We introduced ourselves to one another while at work one night. Ben was the head cook, and he did a great job. The food he made was always hot and freshly prepared, promptly coming out. He made my job as waitress easier. Fast, good food equals great tips.

Many things changed that year. While living in my apartment without any furniture, I slept on an egg cushion for a year. Thanks to Walter my neighbor, who brought it over to me. I did not have all the luxuries I had at home, or even those at Josie's house. I was, however, on my own, paying my bills, living the life. I enjoyed being independent and carefree, but I was not. On several occasions, I went to go to Josie's to get food. I had enough money for the apartment and utilities. That was it. As a result, I lost a lot of weight, which made me feeling good about who I was.

The divorce between my parents became final. I received a large brown envelope in the mail, and in it contained the entire file outlining the approval. It had to have been forty pages in length. I found out from Henry, we all got the same envelope. Even though it was big news, I handled it fairly well. I did repeat to myself, *I guess they really will not get together. Mom has Steve.* I grew to realize my dad was mentally incapable of living alone in society again.

I did give thought to going into the service at that time. I had leaned toward the Air Force, even going to the local recruiting center in Knoxville. There I found out about college opportunities, and a signing bonus. That interested me. I could go to school and *get smart.* So, I signed up. Ben trumped going into the service though. I was a month away from being eighteen and he was twenty-five. I watched how Ben was sweet, funny, and very kind. I observed him with Mr. Cole, the restaurant manager. Mr. Cole was an older gentleman, and Ben had respect for him. That appealed to me. I loved older people and always seemed to gravitate toward them, so I liked how he treated Mr. Cole so respectfully.

Ben and I began dating in October of 1984 and had a relationship for the next year. I can recall, to a tee, the day I lost my virginity. We were going to Ben's parents' cabin for a date. I was so excited to be going out with him, I only imagined what the night was about to hold. We sat in the backyard on a picnic table drinking beer and chasing away bats. I thought they were going get wrapped up in my hair; they were so close. After being intimate with Ben, my immediate thought was, *What would grandma and grandpa say?* I was, after all, living on my own. I was able to vote, and I was paying my own bills, so in my eyes, I was being an adult. I began realizing I did not have to appease anybody, only myself. I had taken photos with my sister's cat, right before leaving for the date. When I look at those pictures now, it is amazing. I have a smile come over me face.

Months had gone by, and I never met Ben's family. No mom or dad, not even his sister or brother. I had met his best friend Matt, and his girlfriend, Abby. We even hung out with them a time or two. To me, it was not really a big deal, but to my sister, Josie, she saw red flags everywhere. She openly referred to him as "Ben the Ripper." But, reflecting back, she never gave me advice or told me why she referred to Ben that way. I knew his friends to be honest, so I did not really think meeting his family meant a lot to me. Josie was mean, never really allowing me to have the spotlight. Since she claimed to be so educated, why not school me?

Ben taught me a lot about the south and how they did things. If it snowed, everything came to a halt. The mountains and steep hills did not allow for good driving conditions. I learned that quickly, because his car was a stick shift, so the hills took some finagling. Ben taught me how to jump-start a car with a clutch and *how not to drive* in the mountains. I felt I was loved, by the way he taught me things. I never had a man take time to teach me anything, except for Uncle Ian and Steve. Both men took me under their wings, even though it had been for a short amount of time. Growing up without my father in the home had a lasting impact on my psyche.

With Ben and our coworker friends, I tried smoking weed for the first time. I also swore I would never do that. After all, my family would scold me. I did not want confrontation of any kind. I got high on weekends and partied with my *friends*. We were drinking and smoking weed regularly. The feeling of getting high was freeing, and felt calming and relaxing to me. I did not understand why at the time. I had selectively chosen to put aside the horrible things I endured growing up. I had a boyfriend, I was living in my own apartment, and really thought it was all a piece of cake. I envisioned it as being what I wanted, when in reality that was only what I *had*. It felt off because it was.

Ben and I took weekend trips to the Smokey Mountains, staying at the Howard Johnson. The rooms' view always faced the rocky river. Ben and I ordered in for room service, which felt very grown-up. I was new at the art of dating. I thought that is how it went when you were being romantic! Romantic my eye! As the saying goes, instincts do not lie. In my case, I was right on. I was no longer the fool because I was aware, and I did not stand for it any longer. I began to realize I was being hidden from his family, friends, and the public. That was a horrible realization to my heart and mind. Why would Josie not tell me that? I rationalized it as being an age difference.

Ben began hanging out less and less. He was spending his time off with his brother and their friends, watching football. The New England Patriots were his team, and I was never invited. I did not really have an issue with it at first. Soon, though, it became clear to me, Ben was not coming around as much because I was wise to him, and because he was using me. I most definitely was not having any part of that. I was convenient and willing, and I did not question him in any way throughout our relationship. What more could I have given to him? I gave him the relationship guys only dream of. I was so utterly inexperienced. I did, however, come to my senses, breaking it off with Ben. He was not fun any longer, and he was not ready to make a commitment to me. I was inconsolable, so I decided to return to Michigan.

> "Keep on, then, seeking first the kingdom, and his righteousness, and all other things will be added to you." So never be anxious about the next day, for the next day will have its own anxieties. Each day had enough of its own troubles.
> —Matthew 6:33–34

CHAPTER 15

I moved back onto Syracuse, in good ol' Detroit. A tremendous amount of change had occurred in one year. Our mayor had given up on our city, and it was slowly falling to the wayside. There were drugs, openly sold and used, at what used to be Bernie's Bar. The parking lot had turned into a seedy place to walk past. The corner hangout on Mound and Lantz was no longer mine. It became a drug hub. Grandma and Grandpa B, Mr. Frank the baker, and Mr. Frank from the dry cleaners were all gone. The neighborhood had deteriorated, and many of the people I used to visit had simply moved out, or they passed away.

I was staying upstairs in the bungalow now and cried a lot for Ben. I could not understand why. Then the realization hit me. Who did I have around me who actually stayed? I was a true wanderer in my mind. I did, however, now occupy the upstairs living area. I considered the Air Force once again and signed up in downtown Detroit. I was to leave in two weeks for boot camp. When two weeks came, I went to the recruiting station, and I was told my weight was too heavy. Five pounds over! "Come back next week," the recruiter said. I never lost the weight, instead I gained. When my mom walked in from work and I was home, she commented, "I knew you didn't have it in you." She was so negative with me, never encouraging her baby.

One of the first people I visited upon returning back to Michigan was Paul's mom, Mrs. Holbrook. We sat outside in her rose garden crying together. I apologized for not making it to the funeral. She was gracious and understanding. Paul never had a chance, she told me. Once they got in, it was an aggressive tumor, robbing Paul of his future in the priesthood. I was beside myself with grief all over again.

In the Fall, I ventured out to Mount Olivet Cemetery in search of Paul's headstone. After finding it, I did, from that day forth, take care in planting flowers every spring. I loved my friend, and now he was forever gone. Paul was the first person in my life to ever die, and I was heartbroken. While at the cemetery, I looked up all of my family members from both my dad and mom's sides. It became a therapy of sorts for me to garden at the sites.

There were good points to moving back to Michigan. Mom and Steve were together all the time. Leslie moved out with her high school sweetheart, Patrick. Danny had left for Florida, and was being mentored by our brother John, so I had the house to myself. I kept it meticulous, and my mom did not have to worry about anything. Once she came home from work, she was able to relax. Steve and mom were on opposite shifts, so evenings she was at home. It was quite a life for me, living in a nice house and not paying any bills. I was working, spending my own cash, and hanging out with Whitney as much as possible. Elizabeth was missing in action, and I had no way of finding her.

I did, years and years later, realize the setup at home was not a benefit to me in anyway. I was taught to expect things to be given to me because I asked. Except now, I was noticing my family did not communicate with me much. They especially were not there when I needed to borrow money for Paul's wake. I had not forgotten that. I knew how to be self-sufficient, but without real responsibilities. All the things I was taught helped to keep a house clean and stay organized. I never learned about money or how to balance a checkbook. I was not taught how to be an independent person. Those were neither helpful nor logical lessons for my mom to have omitted in teaching me. I earned my money, working at an A&P grocery store, and again, I never paid a bill. I was nineteen.

Coming home was fun. Whitney and I went bar hoppin' quite a bit. Gratiot, north of 8 Mile, was the usual spot. Drinking was legal for us also. I danced, flirted, and on occasion got lucky in the back of the car. Ben broke my heart, and I was definitely rebounding. I knew it too, but thought I was just having a good time, like a nineteen-year-old would. The boys I attracted always had condoms. I never worried about protection. If he did not have one, no sex was had. Remember? "If you come home pregnant, I'll disown you." Enough said!

I never brought a boy home to have sex, even though I had plenty of opportunities. My mom was always at Steve's on the weekends. I respected her a great deal, and I never wanted to do something to gain her disapproval. Having sex? Well, she may have been disappointed in that; however, I was stretching my wings and having fun. That was something she never had the opportunity to do. At my age, my mom was getting ready to elope with my dad, and at twenty she was pregnant.

I loved being alone in my own thoughts and never got bored. I simply wrote poems and songs to occupy my mind. Whitney and I continued to be inseparable for the next year. It was not what I wanted to do though. I packed up my belongings again, moving back to Knoxville. I never found a spot where I felt needed, and I missed my niece Brenda tremendously. I returned to the mother-in-law apartment and immediately became employed at a new restaurant chain on Merchant Road. They had great food, and it was easy to sell the menu. Plus, being it was a new restaurant chain, people were excited to try it out.

While working at the restaurant, I met Julie, a fellow waitress. We became instant friends, and she was very funny. Nineteen also, Julie was married to Josh, and they lived on Inskip, walking distance from Josie's home. Josh worked for US Steel in Pittsburg, Pennsylvania, and the plant relocated to Knoxville. Julie was working there part-time. I quickly asked about an open position and was hired immediately afterward. Now I worked two jobs again, and considered getting an apartment of my own. Until then, I was not going to curtail my fun, even though I lived in the mother-in-law apartment.

I met fabulous people wherever I went, and US Steel was no different. I worked with and began dating Phil Tuck. Approximately two months into the relationship, Phil, in my opinion, displayed a sinister side to his character. In the beginning, there were many good laughs and lots of sex. We even went to *The Rocky Horror Picture Show* together. He did undoubtedly become a temptation from Satan. Before long, I witnessed the evil firsthand.

Phil was a fascinating guy, that is why I dated him. He was interested in the unknown, however. The unknown, as in heaven and hell. He was a believer in witchcraft. I dabbled with it in thought only. I never did dive into the things he demonstrated to me. I believed in my God, the Almighty. No one was going to step up and change that, least of all the devil. Phil had an envelope he had sealed with wax at Penn State a few years back. Everything about it was authentic: the date, Phil's initials, and the wax stain and seal. Even the devil himself turned out to be real. I never doubted Satan existed, but did not know the extent of his wrath.

I walked around for three months, three exceeding long months, with a black cloud over my head. It had been directly after the unveiling of the envelope. We had planned to open it that evening, but that did not occur while I was there. God Himself told me to back off that night and during those ninety days. I unequivocally did. I never wavered from God again. Never. God tested me after that several times, and I believe I passed every exam.

Several months after that, I was working at US Steel and got my glove caught in a threading machine. I had my finger sitting on the top of my hand. It was beyond scary. I briskly walked over to Phil, and he escorted me to the office. I was in shock, so Joe the manager, along with Julie, swept me off to St. Mary's Hospital. They announced a broken pinky and a severely dislocated ring finger as their diagnosis. After that incident, I was left alone. I took it as a sign. I love God and only God. I will never be fascinated with Satan again. Witchcraft equals Satan.

The restaurant was getting slow, and business was dying during the day. I only stayed at US Steel a few months after returning to work from my injury. It was too stressful operating the same machine. I was afraid to do my job and began having panic attacks. After my accident, they changed glove policy for that machine; however, it did not matter to me.

I quit both jobs and went to work at Eastown Mall in retail at a full-service pet store. I had saved a little cash and phoned my brother John in Florida. I asked if he could float me a loan for a car. He lent me seven hundred and fifty dollars. I will never forget that feeling. He cared and truly loved me. I knew it. I went the next day and picked up the car I had my eye on.

At the pet store, I was taking care of and selling full-bred dogs. In addition, they had an array of animals looking for loving homes. We sold cats and fish, snakes and tarantulas, exotic birds, and gerbils. I even handled ferrets for the first time. I loved my job, and the animals gave unconditional love to me, never letting me down. There I met Rhoda, a very Southern girl. We became quick friends and were party buddies. She was a few years older than me, but that did not matter. We became close friends, sharing everything, except our men. Never that. With Rhoda, I learned the girlfriends code of ethics. "You never ever date your friend's guy or ex-guy." They are referred to as "sloppy seconds".

On a particular day, I had a customer come in searching for a simple gerbil cage. I sold him a gerbil condo before he left the store. He seemed to have chatted with me for quite a while that afternoon, introducing himself as Adam, then asked for my number. I will not lie, I was excited, excited, excited; he was not like Ben at all. Adam was a twenty-one-year-old, sweet-sounding gentleman. He was tall, dark, and handsome, and a veteran of the armed services. Wow! He swept me off my feet. I, at that point, believed I had fallen in love at first sight. I had instant butterflies. Adam was a decent individual. I knew it instinctively.

Soon, he and I became a couple and dated exclusively. Adam played the piano, harmonica, and guitar. I was enamored by his talents. Adam took me out on several dates before introducing me to his parents. They were lovely people who raised lovely children. Adam's mom was German and had a wonderful accent. She was warm, kind, and invited me in with open arms, literally. His dad was a streaker. I kid you not. He never did it in front of me; he was a pleasant man to converse with. Adam had two sisters who were equally welcoming. Patty was a year younger than me, and Beth, four years older. I felt like part of a family unit. Adam's family was different in many ways. They communicated for one. Watching the dynamics of a loving family can bring a person to tears.

I realized with Adam and his family, that the world was bigger than me, and Michigan. I had been in my little cubical of a spot, and I was not allowed to grow. Yes, I grew taller and filled out as a girl; however, mentally, my family never instructed me on the growth of independence. I was not prepared for all of *life*. Why did they neglect to teach me that? After all, Leslie, Josie, and the boys got that. Why had I not been instructed?

Adam and I celebrated Christmas together that year. The gifts poured out for both of us, and a fabulous celebration was had. The following spring, Easter was spent in Michigan, meeting Whitney and my family.

Looking back now, I wonder what Adam thought of them? I wonder how he looked at me after meeting them. Perhaps that was the weak link in the relationship.

My mom has no tact as a person, and she filtered nothing that came from her mouth. Steve helped her at times, but when a person is grown, sometimes you have to let them make a fool of themselves, and she did. During the visit, I had an inkling my mom told Adam I needed someone to take care of me. Yes! I never did confirm it, but I felt my instincts where right on. Adam and I seemed to have a good relationship. I could see myself marrying him. Truth be told, Adam taught me so much. I grew to embrace the thought that *everything happens for a reason, and in divine order*. I *had not* at that time.

The summer following, Adam came over to talk to me. That night is etched in my mind. He was such a gentleman with the delivery on breaking it off with me, holding me as I sobbed. Adam was a real man, in every sense of the word. He explained how he was not in love with me and did not feel it was fair for either of us to continue dating. He was looking for a wife, and I was not the woman God intended for him. I was devastated once again and thought, *Will I ever find a man as decent as Adam?*

I again loaded my belongings, this time into Adam's truck, and he drove me back to Michigan. Adam and I said goodbye the following morning, after a night of goodbye love. That was the last time I saw his face in person. I could not bear the thought of staying in Knoxville. I knew it was my final trip back *home*. I knew I would never go back to Tennessee, except to visit.

Coming home was not the same. We did not drive to Detroit; we went to the suburbs. That is where Steve and mom bought their home together. The house in Detroit did not belong to us anymore. My mom sold it for thirty-two thousand dollars. I did not blame her or Steve; I was actually happy for them. I was sad for me though. The neighborhood had spoiled to the point that people were moving out in groves. My mom got out at the right time. There were dealers selling drugs right on our corner and all around the blocks. It was clearly not home any longer. More horrible news was Lonesome had to be put to sleep. He was unable to carry on any longer due to his age. It was not a very happy return. I was despondent for weeks.

Mom and Steve's new home was very nice. It was far from Detroit, but that was their goal. Country roads and farmland surrounded their subdivision. It was quite beautiful! The backyard backed up to a forest. It was not the city. Their house was quaint…peaceful…serene. I moved in with them both, but I faced a bit of difficulty. I was already on my own. I was only twenty years old but had freedom under my belt. To move into someone else's space was going to be a challenge in my mind, and it was. Steve was welcoming, but my mom was continuously rude to me. I do not think she wanted me there. I felt Steve most likely coaxed my mom into letting me come. I was a great daughter; there was not one reason why my mom should not want me to stay.

Although I was welcomed to stay with them, I knew in my heart it was Steve's convincing that made that happen, and that made it harder to swallow, I cannot lie. It was Steve's home too. No more Syracuse, no more Detroit, no more family home. Everything was gone in a matter of a year. I never said "goodbye" to the Detroit home. No closure was had.

Finding work was easy for me. My last employment was working for a hotel on Merchant Road back in Knoxville. I provided housekeeping to the guests and soon was promoted to a front desk clerk and transporter. From there, I was promoted again and became the night auditor. So that is where I began once home. I soon gained employment at the Knights Inn. I worked as both a desk clerk and a night auditor, realizing I enjoyed mathematical problem solving.

Chad was my boss, and a great soul. The job I had now was by far my favorite. I felt a great connection to the work I was doing, and soon found myself excelling in the auditing field. Remember, C student! I did, on occasion, meet guests who were checking in for the night. After work, I ended up in their rooms. Sex was fun to me, but I did it more so because I longed for love.

Mom and Steve finally got married. It was a very small justice of the peace ceremony, and I do not recall any of the siblings being invited. There was a large turnout for their reception at a restaurant on Anchor Bay. They had been together since I was nine, and after eleven years, they made it an official union. I loved and respected Steve a lot. I wanted to call him dad, but he was not comfortable with that. He explained how I had a dad, and Steve was a friend to me. After all these years, Steve *was* my dad. I accepted the friendship, but in my heart, I called him my father. He was, after all, there for me while I grew and matured. He was an awesome role model and taught me the meaning of second chances.

Steve and I had a change in our relationship while living under his roof. He had, for all intents and purposes, become my dad. Even though Steve was there for me while I grew up, he was perhaps a bit uncomfortable giving his opinion. I believe when my mom married him, he then took on the role as my parent silently. I was elated. Steve treated me differently than that of my siblings. He nurtured me.

I saw after all those years, he was still listening to and reading Dr. Wayne Dyer. I was fascinated and my interests were piqued. I was not an excellent reader, but I did enjoy learning. The books I had read to that point were required by school. Steve introduced me to a genre of self-help books, tapes, and resources. His favorite motivational speaker was Dr. Dyer though, mine became Brian Tracy. I watched as those tapes and books made a transformation in Steve. He was softer around the edges and wanted to teach me what he learned. I let him do just that.

From here on out, Steve not only instructed me; he taught and fortified me. I honestly never received that from my mom. I wondered if perhaps my other siblings, my sisters in particular, missed out too. I watched them, though they did not seem to struggle like me. They were with their boyfriends and had what they wanted, so it appeared. I also received quite a bit of teaching from John. He was a mover and shaker in Florida, dealing with real estate and investments. John learned his techniques by listening to money-building tapes and CDs. I gathered information from him and began working on my self-esteem.

My mom and Steve were still working at Chrysler on opposite shifts. I really loved that. I cleaned the house, so my mom did not have to worry about it. I scrubbed the bathrooms and showers, washing the floors on my hands and knees, just like my grandma taught me. It was my pay, in my mind, for living there, since they did not ask for any money. My mom and I appeared to have the utmost affection and love for each other; however, something was missing. I never felt completely loved or validated. Whew! Validation was a big one. However, I soon clung to Steve's advice, and that held my head above the water. The small techniques he taught proved to be extremely helpful as I grew older.

> Faith is the assured expectation of what is hoped for, the evident demonstration of realities that are not seen.
> —Hebrews 11:1

CHAPTER 16

In September of 1987, I had only been home for four months, and I was still pining for Adam. I helped myself to get over him by hooking up with male guests at the hotel. I was inadvertently raised to either take or leave a man. I wanted a boyfriend, but knew I was going about it in the wrong manner. A semi-permanent guest came into the office one evening to settle his long-standing bill. Randy had another man with him, Peter. Randy introduced him as his cousin. I had seen Randy before and was taken in by his bad-boy ways. Soon though, I learned he was married, and his wife was expecting in November. Quickly and suddenly, it became "Randy who?" Pete lived a couple of cities away in Eastpointe. Randy had a house fire, so Pete and Randy were at the hotel until they finished remodeling the home. I was intrigued with their handyman ways. My brother John dabbled with wood and painting, similar to what these two men were taking on. I flirted with Pete, and he flirted with me, kind of.

Pete was not sure of himself, and that did not appeal to me. However, I struck up a conversation with him. He was tall and fit, with blond hair and blue eyes. He appeared to be a hard worker, with excellent work ethics at his job as a glass installer. One evening, Pete came in and started talking with me. We chatted for a long time while I worked. He asked what time I got done for the night. We got together at eleven in the evening, staying up till 4:30 the following morning. We discussed a lot with one other, talking about a plethora of subjects. A few weeks later, Pete and I became a couple. Months later, it dawned on me, his name was Pete, the same name I prayed for as a young girl. I could not help but think he may be the man I marry.

We had tons of fun together for the first few weeks. Going to Metro Beach in the middle of the day was a one-time treat. Pete never took off from work, but that particular day, he decided to play hooky. We walked the beach together and chatted hour after hour. I learned how his father had just passed away in February, and as if that was not enough, Pete had just had a break up too. He had been with Anna for many years and had recently found her cheating on him. Pete explained some of the dynamics of his family and six siblings. He was an identical twin to Patrick (Paddy). There were four additional brothers and one sister in his family.

I met Paddy one afternoon while I was at work. He and Pete *were* identical. Wow! I had never known, nor had I seen identical twins before. I knew within five minutes, though, their personalities were not the same. *Thank God*, I thought. I felt uneasy and uncomfortable with Paddy. Not in a bad way. Paddy was, however, an extremely negative guy. He complained about anything, and it appeared he found happiness in nothing.

I received a call from Whitney upon returning home. She was crying on the phone, with news to share. Whitney had been dating Brad, and they both were going to have a baby. The wedding was being planned. I was scared for her. I did not know Brad, and I had no way of knowing what kind of man he was, or if he would take care of Whitney. They had a small shower and exchanged vows in a church in Sterling Heights. It was a beautiful ceremony, and I was her maid of honor. Brad and Whitney eventually moved into an apartment, welcoming into the world a healthy baby boy, Brad Jr. Life was busy for Whitney, and I did not have an inkling to the pressures she must have felt being a new mom and wife. We chatted less and less.

Two months after meeting Pete, I moved into the home he shared with Paddy and his girlfriend, Mara. I could not see myself at Steve and my mom's anymore. My mom, more than Steve, got bent out of shape about my coming home late after work one night. She also implied the cleaning of my space was not to her specifications. I was there less and less anyway because I felt the need to move on. My mom made it easy too. She actually encouraged me to move out when I told her of my plans. I felt that bad, coming from her. She should not have wanted me living in sin, so I had thought.

The arrangement of moving in with Pete was not without apprehensiveness on my part. I never felt connected to the space at Pete's house in any way. It was an eerie feeling comparable to when I was growing up in Detroit. There were many parties and fun nights there, but I never felt comfort. I resented Mara a lot. Pete, Paddy, and I did all the cleaning. She did very little unless coaxed into participating with us.

Mara was a very unmotivated individual who never worked a job. She did sell perfume door-to-door at some point, but never working to collect a tax return. I was working two jobs, contributing to the bills and food, while Mara was filing her nails for hours on end. She never prepared food for us or cleaned up after a meal, often locking herself in the bathroom during our dinner's prep time. It was Pete, Paddy, and I who cooked and cleaned. I was not used to living in that manner; I was used to hard work and self-sufficient behavior. In the big picture, there was not one thing I could do to change her or the situation. Paddy seemed irritated but content! After all, he yelled at her and degraded her, and she never changed. *Red flag!*

Pete and Paddy were great in the kitchen and around the grill. They were also avid fishermen. They brought home about twenty, three-foot lake salmon that Fall. We ate a lot of fresh fish and froze a great amount. I watched the two of them fillet every one of those salmon. It was really something to see. They effortlessly skinned and cleaned all the fish in record time. The bellies of the females were filled with eggs. Wow! I was in awe. I had only been fishing as a child; I had never seen what I was experiencing. Paddy got the cheesecloth out, and Pete made little egg sacks for bait. The whole process was very intriguing. They used those sacks to fish for more salmon the following weekend.

I enjoyed going to Lexington with them just to hang out and watch. On occasion, I did cast a pole. It really was exciting to see how the egg sacks were used. Pete and Paddy learned a lot from their dad and brothers; I was learning so much from them. The twins were highly intelligent with whatever they touched. They never thought that of themselves. I wondered why they both had such little self-esteem.

November was closely approaching. It was the first time I made a turkey for the holiday dinner. I had just turned twenty-one years old at the beginning of the month. I was cooking for eight people, and to that point in my young life, I had only watched my mom during the process. Yes, I helped her, but that consisted of my chopping vegetables. I knew the steps in my head after all, because I did observe my mom every year. So, I took a deep breath and cooked. The turkey was juicy and delicious, but the gravy had very little flavor. I made a call to my mom to help fix it. She snidely said to me, "You're actually cooking?" My meal was a success!

I never knew why Mara did not like me, but I found out that night. Pete's ex-girlfriend Anna and Mara were best friends since grade school. I did not understand why Mara was hateful toward me. But when it comes to situations such as that, there are many times, no rhyme or reason. I peacefully stayed away from her after that, examining her from a distance. Mara was immature, often acting like a teenager. She displayed inappropriate behavior, and I felt uncomfortable around her every time she drank.

I ignorantly began giving thought to others' lives instead of taking care of my own. I wondered what in the world Paddy saw in Mara. She was, in my opinion, a lazy drunkard who refused to cook, clean, or work. I was raised to believe "cleanliness is next to Godliness." She was neither, which was a surprise, because Mara was Polish Catholic, like me. I believed I was too much of a social butterfly for her liking. We were cordial to one other when we spoke, but that got old very quickly. I never encountered anyone like Mara before. In addition, I had never been a fan of folks who think they are better than me, or those who talk behind my back. I had plenty of that growing up, and I was not about to take it now. I always seemed to have people in my life who acted like they cared, but in actuality they did not. Mara was a bad actress.

I was employed at a Red Roof Inn as a desk clerk and auditor by now. The job was a move up from the last hotel, and I was in a better position to becoming a manager. That was ultimately my goal. I was hoping on a scholarship now, for many had become available. I was working the night shift and reading the *Detroit Free Press* obituary section. There was a name I recognized, a high school mate. I began to immediately cry and called Whitney. It was 10:00 p.m. I explained what had happened and who passed away. Whitney was preoccupied and was not really listening. I sensed a detachment in her voice. What the hell was going on? Whitney and I knew each other very well. I never found out what the issue was, but for whatever reason, Whitney and I did not speak after that. I figured that was what happened once you got married and had children. I was not happy.

Christmas was at both Pete's moms' home and at my grandparents. It worked out well because Pete's mom had Christmas Eve and my grandma,

Christmas Day. I sent a card to Whitney's mom and dad's house, never receiving a response from her.

Pete's mom, Mrs. Abby, was a delightful woman to me. She was hospitable and friendly, always having a smile to give. I helped her, both during and after the meal, with food preparation and cleanup. It was something she obviously did not expect. I assisted in cleaning the dishes, throwing the wrapping papers out, and stoking the fire. I observed that none of the other ladies helped to clean, except Pete's sister, Nora, and Lucy, his sister-in-law. It became obvious who the helpers were and who were the ones with their hands out for the food and gifts. Sadly, I am being honest.

Pete's mom appreciated me that evening, and I appreciated her, along with her amazing food. She prepared dinner for over thirty adults and ten children. That was a large amount of cooking and setup time. She was an extraordinary cook. Mrs. Abby bought me a baby blue sweater that year. I wore it all the time, finally discarding it some years later, after it had worn out. I really liked Pete's mom, and I grew to love her as a person.

Pete's family was a little off. They were loud, obnoxious, and clearly racists. They referred to blacks openly in the same manner as my mom. My skin crawled every time I thought of their upbringing. I had a hard time with their outspokenness around me. I came to see Pete's family and my family run together in their dysfunction. In addition, they were a lot like my born-into family. Before long though, I grew comfortable in Mrs. Abby's household, and with being around the siblings. I did speak my mind but always in a polite way. My mind did not match with theirs at all. We were all on a different plateau, just like my family. However, I never let that intimidate me. I just kept on smiling and being me. I realized it was the technique I used while growing up. I could not go on being silent any longer. My lips wanted to repute every racist comment they said.

At the time, it was a sad and trauma-filled time for me. My cat since childhood, Tabby, was put to sleep by my mom. I was devastated. Tabby was diabetic, and Steve gave her shots every day. She just could not hold on any longer, so my mom put her down. I let my mom know what kind of discord I was in by calling her a "killer." She, of course, was not. I just did not understand the complexity of the situation. I have come to know firsthand the stress involved in putting an animal down. I had to forgive myself for saying that to my mom, and I apologized to her. I was wrong! Instead of forgiving me, I got the cold shoulder. She never explained *anything* to me. It was a shortcoming of hers and was now easily picked up on. Wow! That was a pivotal moment for me, realizing my mom had additional faults. I never believed in her way of thinking, but I chalked that up to us being different people. I never thought she did not know. I thought my mom was perfect. She was very far from it.

    I have come to realize, as children, we look up to our parents in an adoring way. We must see, though, they are merely human beings, just as we are. They too are on a journey of learning. When you are raised a certain way, I believe we will either gravitate to that lifestyle or we will run from it.

> If anyone says, "I love you God," and yet is hating his brother,
> he is a liar. For the one who does not love his brother whom
> he has seen, cannot love God whom he has not seen.
>
> —1 John 4:20

CHAPTER 17

The following Spring, I began to feel very comfortable with the way Pete was treating me, even though it was not healthy. His snide comments were something I was definitely used to. After all, my family was consistently the same way. In fact, my family was continuing to do it to me, but in a completely different way. My family guilt-tripped and shamed a person, and then they talked behind their back. But something in me was different. I did not like nor did I feel comfortable engaging in conversations with those personality types. But what was I going to do? It was my family. I loved them, just not their minds, actions, or personalities. In my opinion, that leaves *nothing. What was I doing with Pete?*

Sometimes, even when people are verbally attacking you, you do not think you can do better, or because it is second nature, you accept the behavior. Somehow their stabs at you become acceptable, even though they are personal. Your self-esteem starts to melt away, if you had any. Before you catch it, you may become subservient to what is uncomfortable. One must recognize that for what it is. It is an extremely unhealthy way to exist. I believe it is a conscious decision to continue to live in that manner. The way I got treated was not my doing by any means. I was merely attracting what I knew. However, choosing to stay is a choice.

There were times of verbal assaults toward me, and attacks against my family, by Pete. The family attacks bothered me a lot, although it was all true. I did not want to admit my shortcomings to Pete, or myself for that matter. The way my family treated me was wrong, but I still loved them, out of obligation. There was a code in my family: We all stuck up for each other, no matter what. That is not a bad thing if you have equal comradery with those same individuals. I did not though. My siblings never protected me in any way. I longed for a conversation with Whitney. I sent another card to her parents, but no response came.

Pete took it too far one day with the insults toward me as we were driving back home after attending a party. I ask him repeatedly to pull the truck over, but he laughed, refusing to slow down, and I became infuriated. At nearly thirty-five miles an hour, I jumped, tucked, and rolled out of that truck, landing on the grass easement. I was livid at Pete. I walked two miles back to the home we shared, the entire time planning on how I was going to exit the relationship. Within a week, I moved out into my own apartment, in Hamtramck, a little Polish community in the middle of Detroit. I was bound and determined to teach Pete a lesson. After dating for two years, the relationship was going nowhere. I began to play hard-to-get. My mom and siblings taught me how to bestow guilt onto people. So that is how I thought I could change Pete.

My family all seemed to be doing well emotionally, except for me. They obviously learned something I had not. I was dating my mom in Pete. I was crystal clear on that. Then it hit me like a ton of lead! My mom was waiting for me to meet a man who would marry me, ultimately taking care of me. She had me messed up. I did not *need* any man taking care of me. I was making great money working. I did not need *any* man. I always grew up with the idea of having my man to accentuate my personality, not make it. I have no recollection of how that belief came to be; I just knew it fit me. I was not comfortable with my weight or anger at the time, but everything else, I loved.

Pete's brother, Rick, was married to Lucy. Rick's former wife and he had a daughter, Emily. He and Lucy did not have any children together. Often, they hosted parties in their yard for all to come and enjoy. Pete invited me to the Annual Oyster Bash of 1989, being held at Rick and Lucy's house. It was a party atmosphere, and Mrs. Abby was not there, so the "boys" let loose. I enjoyed being with certain brothers. Rick was one.

I proceeded to doll up in my nicest dress to go to a jean-wearing party. I was honestly laying in my bed when Pete called that night. I explained to Pete how I had been on a date to a wedding and was coming in the clothes I was wearing. It was a little lie in the big picture to see if he was still interested. That is called "trial ballooning." It is the preface of giving out a tad bit of information to see if you will achieve a particular result you are looking for, better known as manipulation. It was not my usual style, but I had learned the technique off of a self-help cassette. I really thought Pete was the one, that is why I did that. What I missed, though, was the fact that we were not compatible, yet I pursued him.

The night of the party, I ended up spending the night at Pete and Paddy's house. I woke up the next morning to use the restroom, and I was sincerely taken aback. There was a contraceptive sponge in the garbage can, and it was used. I knew it was not Mara's, so I confronted Pete. Casey, from his work, and he apparently got it on while he was *not* pining away for me. *Crushed.* I was crushed! It had been the afternoon before, when Pete was with her; now he was having sex with me? *What a discussing pig,* I thought.

Pete did tell me he had been with Casey a few times, but that it meant nothing to him. I wondered if that had also occurred in the last two years; I was sure it had. He said he wanted me though, and that was music to my ears. Being that Pete was so believable, we began dating again. I obviously thought it would be different. *Red flag!* There is a quote in the mental health field: "If you keep doing the same behavior, but you expect a different result, that is the definition of insanity." I expected to see a change. Oh, Pete was sincere. He never dated Casey again, as far as I knew. However, one has to want to change, to make a difference in their behavior, in order to be successful at becoming different. I, nor Pete, knew that fact, so how were we to do it? In addition to changing, one must first recognize there is, in fact, a personal need for change and growth.

Paddy and Mara were always in attendance at Rick's parties too. Mara always got intoxicated. She was tall and thin; a small amount of liquor produced a quicker result for her than the rest of us. She also made a spectacle of herself when she drank. Why, at that point in my life, was I surrounded by alcoholics? Yes, Pete's family and the in-laws were alcoholics. Mara, when drunk or high, literally hung on you, dragging your shoulder to the ground. She also acted as if we were great buddies. *Sloppy drunks are unattractive,* I thought. I myself do not admire, let alone befriend, the enemy. I like to keep them at a distance. Little did I know; I was about to be infiltrated by them.

Mara and Paddy were also using cocaine on a consistent basis. Paddy had a connection with Mo working at the glass company. Mo was their supplier. Before long, I was trying it, compliments of Mo. We frequented his house in the city, on Connor and I-94. Even back then, it was a horrible area of Detroit. Paddy never introduced me to the drug, but Mara and Pete did. As we sat in Mo's basement, it was Mara saying, "It will make you feel sooo good," "It will take you away." Pete smiled, not responding. Well, let me say, it takes you away all right. It takes you to the bank, leaving you broke. Pete and I did the cocaine together, with Paddy and Mara as well. I, at the time, remember feeling horribly guilty, wondering what my grandparents would think. I reasoned with myself, *It's not like I'm an addict. We're just having fun.* I repeated that quietly in my head.

We did have fun, but the next day, Paddy had to go get more. Consciously, I was craving more cocaine. It was the first time I had ever tried a major drug, and cocaine had a completely different effect then marijuana. Weed relaxed me, but cocaine made me feel like I had to be on the move. By the way, the big lie is that cocaine is a motivator. No way. It is not a motivator, but it is a thief. In my mind, it got me up and moving. True, it does do that. However, you also crash. Mine came at 7:30 a.m., and I will tell you it is a rough feeling! After that horrible experience of coming down from the high, you only want more. Cocaine is a very addictive drug; one I refer to as "the never-ending roller coaster."

Pete and I went to a party at Connie and JoJo's one Saturday evening. JoJo and Pete were high school buddies. It was exciting to learn how to playing euchre that night. Along with card playing, there included *a lot* of cocaine. It was spread out on the kitchen counter for anyone to help themselves to. There had to have been two eight balls laying there alongside the rolled-up twenty-dollar bill. We were partying for a few hours before I realized that Connie and JoJo's children were asleep upstairs. I was internally furious after they mentioned that; however, I did not leave. It most certainly was not acceptable behavior for myself to stay; and it was out of character for me. I longed for the cocaine, but the sensible thing to have done would have been to leave. I wanted to express to Connie why I thought it was wrong to party with your children home. That, of course, was not my place. I am wholeheartedly uncomfortable with myself when I recall that memory.

The following day was a Sunday. I had not been to Mass in a long time. As I lay in Pete's waterbed, I decided I needed to go, and I did. I felt so badly for having stayed at that wretched home. I called it that because I was adamant, at the time, that partying with the children home was a huge faux pas. I went to confession to cleanse my horrible soul. Just because I went to the priest to confess my sins does not mean the partying stopped. Pete and I drank rum and Coke, smoked weed, and snorted cocaine at least twice a month. It was fun, irresponsible, costly, and it was highly addictive too. We were young and having fun. Little did I know what the effects of doing drugs would do to me long-term.

Pete and I occasionally went up north with his high school friends. Ronnie was a hard-core drug user due to a back injury, beginning his addiction to pain pills. Pete and I brought cocaine with us to enjoy for the weekend while we mingled with friends. I had won two tickets for The Who on a local radio station, and I traded them to Elizabeth's first husband for an eight ball. I was not a bad girl, but I was doing bad things. We went up north a few times after that, but Ronnie was a creepy person. He never looked you in the eyes, and he was shady. Ronnie only called when he needed or wanted something from Pete or Paddy. He was what I referred to as a *part-time friend*. In reality, we only went up north to visit Ronnie's parents. Then going up to the cabin ended abruptly. Ronnie was not a good person, and Pete knew it. Something occurred between them, but I till today have no idea what.

Pete and Paddy joined a bowling league together. For the most part, I was asked to go along and cheered them on. It was a time of many fun moments, partying on the weekends, and working hard during weekdays. One night, Pete and I were driving home when he leaned into me, telling me he loved me. I responded back with the same. I felt warm inside. I felt happy and pleased that someone actually loved *me*. Then I wondered *how* he loved me? *Why* did he love me? Those were all questions needing to be asked. I was not sabotaging my own happiness; I was double-checking. Adam and Ben hurt me.

Even though Pete and I had been dating a couple of years, it truly meant nothing. Remember, my mom never taught me about boys or men; no one did. I asked Pete, throughout our courtship, what it was about me he felt he loved the most. He could not pinpoint an answer other than to say "Everything." *Everything?* I was hoping he would elaborate, but Pete never did. That is not the way it should be. If you are dating a person and you say you love them, trust and believe, you better know why.

Pete and I dated for two years before I felt comfortable hugging other members of his family, with the exception of the children. The moment I met them, we were all buddies, hugging each other regularly. Those little people needed positive contact so badly. Plus, children know your intentions. Yes, they do! They are smart and uninhibited with their tongues. Before I came into Pete's family, the children never had any physical loving with each other or any adult. None of the kids heard "I love you" and hugs were not given. I altered their lives. They were not a family who showed affection. Paddy and Pete told me they did not recall the last time their mom said she loved them. I was sad for them. My mom told me all the time.

Mrs. Abby was not outspoken; she was actually quite the opposite. She was tall and thin, refined and ladylike. She was a great mom, sacrificing for all seven of her children. In the '70s, Pete's mom was a cub leader for the Boy Scouts. She was the family trailblazer in many ways. Mrs. Abby made the best German potato salad too, even though she was English and Irish. Her husband, George, was one hundred percent German; Mrs. Abby retained many of their recipes, cooking them frequently. I grew to love her as a woman and a mom because she was genuine. Soon I realized she did not have to say the words I love you; she showed you constantly that she did. My mom never did that for me.

Pete and I were together four years, but living in separate places. He always lived with Paddy since the time of moving out of their parent's home. They truly were inseparable, identical twins. That became another aspect of our relationship that bothered me. Would I ever be good enough to take Paddy's place? I wondered, *Would Pete accept me for me, down the road?* That proved to be very insightful talk I had with myself. Years later, it became a pivotal point for me to prove.

My mother taught me the meaning of hard work, how to worry about what others think of you, and how to be a racist. Only the first of those could be used to live and build a foundation from. I began to see I was a good person, but I had no skills. I fulfilled my mom's prophecy about my ending up to only work menial jobs. She, I adamantly felt, was to blame. I began therapy at that point.

> And he will wipe out every tear from their eyes, and death will be no more, neither will mourning nor outcry, nor pain anymore. The former things have passed away.
>
> —Revelations 21:4

CHAPTER 18

The moment I became twenty-three, I knew my mom did a negligent job preparing me for the skills needed to succeed in adulthood. The actual point being, she did not *teach* me in any way. Aunt Kate did more for me than my own mother. At the time, I was running my own business: a full-service cleaning company. I obtained residential and commercial accounts by advertising and sending business letters out. Cleaning was something I was extremely meticulous at. So, I decided to start making a living doing it, eventually working six days a week, ten hours a day. I cleaned the old Polish way, by scrubbing the floors on my hands and knees. I changed bedsheets, organized and moved furniture. No one in my area was cleaning like I was.

The first few therapists were not a fit for me. Instead of leaving to dredge up my story again, I stayed with them, giving them the benefit of the doubt. That had a massively negative impact on my growth. If you are, for any reason, unsatisfied with your therapist, get a new one. There are a plethora of them available, and many good ones too. The important point to remember is that therapists are people too. They are individuals with their own pasts and are not perfect, nor do they have all the answers. Therapy should be entered into with an open mind, to learn, grow, and mature. Then, with hard work, faith, and perseverance, you will become the person you have always envisioned yourself to be. I will not lie to you; it takes a great deal of will and determination to learn new coping skills.

In the twenty-six years I spent in therapy, I have had close to twenty therapists. There are five whom I consider to have been top-notch in their field. Those individuals, over a period of time, because I was willing, and because they were knowledgeable, changed and transformed my life. Whoever said one person can make a huge difference in your life was correct. That can work both positively or negatively. Those individuals were brought into my life at pivotal moments in time, when I needed answers. Sometimes I prayed for a specific topic to get resolved. I often had them fixed, after prayer and a good night's sleep, having listened to God for guidance. I went to my therapists and asked them for help and instructions on how to improve myself.

My therapy, in the beginning, had much to do with how I felt about my dad's illness, my brother Danny, and my mom's obvious detachment from me. Then came the bigger subjects of Pete and the dynamics of our relationship. He was a fun drunk, up to a certain point. My uncles drank socially, and after all, Pete only drank on weekends. Soon though, that changed.

Pete and I were dating exclusively for five years, and we decided financially, it was a great idea to move in together. After all, we were both paying rent and utilities, car payments, and insurance. We moved into an apartment in Clinton Township. I loved the large and spacious area inside the unit. There was also a built-in swimming pool and tennis courts for the residents. *Wow! Pete and I were living in a palace*, I thought. It was as if my dreams were blossoming.

Looking back and reflecting on that time, I did not even know what love looked like. After all, my parents were not together while I was growing up. My mom and Steve's relationship remained confidential. Yet, I believed I was in love with Pete. To me, love was not perfect. That is where I was wrong. The right love, healthy love, is indeed perfect. Love is always perfect when you are with the right person. Even in the midst of disagreements, you are bound and determined to make it work. It is the individual's personality or their perception of what love is supposed to be that intervenes. Often, it makes love ugly and ultimately makes love die.

Pete and Paddy had their thirtieth birthday party at our new place. It was my idea, so I asked Mara to be a part of the planning. I felt it only right to do that. Mrs. Abby, my mom and Steve, friends and family, all showed up for the festivities. A wonderful time was had by everyone there. I never forgot the total Mara skimped out on paying me though. Eighty-two dollars was her portion. It took a lot for me to get together with her to begin with.

She actually stuck me with the entire one hundred and sixty-five dollars to absorb. I was so livid. It was definitely the principle, not the money, but I let it slide. Approximately one week later, Pete asked about the amount and who paid for all the food and drinks. I told him what happened with Mara, and he was visibly angry. From that point on, Pete began to see for himself what I had seen from day one. He did let it all go and did not mention it again. That was a move my mom used to do to me. *Red flag!*

I considered myself to be a good judge of character. When I meet someone for the first time, I listen to them speak. After about ten minutes, I am able to assess their personality. I do not do that to be arrogant; I do it to protect myself. I had been pulverized over the years, so I refused to let another person try and get one over on me. No way did I allow it. Do not get me wrong; I never set out to judge anyone. In reality, I wanted to protect my mind and heart. That is what is called being proactive for yourself.

Once Pete and I were in the apartment for about a year, out of the blue, Danny invited me out for breakfast. He had a 1965 Fairmont he had just purchased. He wanted to go to eat and take me for a ride, which was out of the ordinary. I agreed, and we shared breakfast at Big Boy Restaurant. At the time, it was all I thought there was to the outing. However, Danny dropped a bomb on me, actually apologizing for having sexually molested me. He said, verbatim, "I was just a stupid kid." I remember thinking, *Is that all you've got?* I remember my response: "It's over and done, we don't have to talk about it." What the hell was I thinking? I wanted to attack him.

I never forgot about the abuse; I did, however, suppress my memories. At the time Danny said that to me, I felt my face flush with heat. I was instantly transported into being little Barbara again. An extremely dirty and disgusting feeling came over my entire being. Yuck! A flashback occurred, and I busted out into tears. Danny said, "Come on, man, don't do that." He thought crying was a sign of weakness, but to me, I had become a helpless little girl again.

We finished breakfast, and Danny took me for a ride through the Grosse Pointe's, on Lakeshore Drive. We drove along the water banks of Lac St. Clair; it was a gorgeous sunny morning. Mansions lined the right side of the street, and I gazed at every one as we passed. Before I knew it, I felt like Barb again, my feelings of *not being in control* had dissipated.

The ride lasted about an hour. Danny's car was nice, although not my style of a classic.

The meeting with my brother made me feel better about the situation; however, Danny was only trying to clear his own conscience. At that point in my life, I had a decent relationship with my family, even Danny. I put everything I felt aside, because they were my family and I needed their love, so I believed. I want to make a point now about this subject. If people are supposed to love you, and they say they do, but their actions are hateful and abusive, you owe it to yourself to find greener pastures. No one should be given authority over you—no one but God. Ask yourself if the love you feel is loving and nurturing. If it is not, get out of the relationship. You will be healthier and much happier for having done so. The initial sadness and loneliness will pass.

During the early '90s, Pete and Paddy were building and racing hydroplanes. They took their boat all around the East Coast, even hitting the scene in Quebec. Partnering with their brother Rick, the three of them built an awesome-sounding and lean-running hydroplane. I went with them on trips, either in the motor home, or we all drove, renting hotel rooms. They were party times, without any doubt. Pete and I could polish down a fifth of rum over the weekend, often finishing an additional pint.

One year, while they were touring with the hydroplane, I opted out of going along. Instead, I went to Port Austin alone to cleanse my soul and hopefully see Aunt Kate and Uncle Ian. I was an adult now. I had not seen them in twelve years. I pitched a tent at the state campgrounds and set off down Spring Street to their home. I remember being nervous, my palms sweaty. Aunt Kate welcomed me in with open arms, inviting me for dinner. I regretfully did not go. I was there for my own soul-searching, but little did I know, God had sent me there for something more. Both the Kay's passed without my seeing them again. I had great remorse over not going back there to break bread with them once again. While camping, I ventured out to visit my weeping willow tree at the convent. As I laid on the ground under the tree, I stared at God above. There, I asked Him to help me. When you ask for something, you must listen intently to whomever is giving you advice. If it is God, you must listen with your spirit.

Once I got back home, I was working my tail off again, cleaning homes and offices. I decided to stretch my networking. I reached out to a friend of

Rick's who owned a marina in St. Clair Shores. I thought if I cleaned brand-new boats, I could multiply my earnings, ultimately working half the time. Each house may yield eighty dollars for a total of five hours per month. I had approximately fifteen residential accounts and ten commercial accounts. If I cleaned a yacht, earning three hundred dollars on the low end for a day's work, I could ideally work less. I called the owner and began working for Connie, detailing their brand-new cruisers.

During that time of busting butt, my sister Leslie and I were having a conversation over coffee at her home. She asked me, "When are you going to get a real job?" *What? She didn't just say that!* I thought. I laid into Leslie, telling her I made more money in one week than her husband Patrick did. I was not being disrespectful in my delivery, although she had been to me. My facts were straight and accurate. She was out of line. That was the beginning of the end with Leslie. She was uptight and inexperienced at working; I was not. I had a lot of jobs growing up; she had two in her lifetime.

My mom was working a lot of overtime. Cleaning her own home was not possible, so I added it to my schedule. My mom knew I was an excellent cleaner, and I loved my job too. Their ranch-styled, spacious living room was gorgeous, and my mom had an eye for modern decorating. I never charged them for cleaning, but she always paid me. My mom was not going to take a handout of any kind, not even from her daughter. I often made my schedule, so I was able to chat with Steve afterward. Simply making some small changes proved to be a wonderful gift of knowledge for me. We sat every week for a minimum of two hours, and Steve schooled me in life. He knew I never received that; he told me so. I had a sudden weight come off of me, one that had been there for years. It was refreshing, to say the least! Steve loved me like a daughter; there was no denying it. I felt elated, I felt loved, and I knew God had not forgotten about my prayers.

I was working less hours and was able to be home most days by three o'clock in the afternoon. I came home to a message on our answering machine from Steve one unforgettable day. My grandpa, who had fallen months earlier, had become ill from his injuries and passed away. I immediately fell to the floor, sobbing for what seemed like hours. I got into the car and drove to tell Pete who was at Mrs. Abby's. I remember it so vividly. As soon as I started driving, "Into the Mystic" by Van Morrison came on the radio. I wept all the while as I listened to Van belt out one of my favorite songs. My heart was heavy, but when the song finished, I felt my grandpa's soul right there in my car with me. Eerie, I know, but it was a comforting feeling.

I walked in the backdoor, only to turn around, walking out. Once Pete saw my face, he ran after me. I explained what the message said, and we cried deeply together. My grandpa was the first major family member to die in my life, and he was the patriarch for all of us. Plans and arrangements were made for the wake. My grandpa had a beautiful service, and many were in attendance. It was surely a tribute to his long and love-filled life.

My grandma was so strong; I never saw her break down. For the first time, I saw many people whom I had not seen in years. Strangers and family broke out into tears at any given moment. As I approached my grandpa, fragrant flowers, plants, and statues engulfed the casket. It was a sign, a moment in time, where I was completely calm. It may have been the rum and coke helping me relax. I had to shake off the thick anxiety I was feeling before entering the funeral home. Pete and I had two drinks each before leaving our apartment for the rosary. My mom had to make her sarcastic comments. Beforehand, I was a wreck. Pete tried nearly everything to calm me, but now calmness, total calmness. God was with me, guarding me. My grandpa, I believe, was in the light of God's love.

I cannot deny the facts. I struggled for two years afterward, missing my grandfather immensely. He was the first man, next to Ian Kay, who represented a strong male figure in my life. I went to visit my grandma all the time after that. We went shopping, usually ending our day with lunch at Big Boy Restaurant. We also shared a love of scrabble. I began getting closer to my grandma, and the time spent together was magical, informative, and educational. I learned many facts about cooking, baking, and loss. I picked my grandma's brain for information, and she willingly taught me.

Pete and I were doing okay for ourselves. I thought after six years of dating, the next thing to do was to get married. I was always the one in the relationship making the first move. As a girl growing up, I never dreamed about my wedding day or honeymoon. I only prayed to have a husband who would love and adore me. I began looking at wedding rings and fantasizing, never bringing the subject up to Pete. Everything was going well for us as a couple in my eyes. The snide remarks remained to come out of Pete's mouth, but I took it in stride. Pete and I had a very tumultuous relationship. At times, I hated the way he treated me, but he always told me he loved me. I thought he did, in his own capacity. Why was that enough for me?

I began believing I did not want to die alone. It was a worrisome thought weighing heavily on my mind. Thinking is one thing; believing is different. I do not remember the first step; I recall only believing I should not die alone. I got my jewelry catalog out and proceeded to peruse the engagement rings section. With scissors in hand, I cut my favorites into little squares. There were perhaps ten different designs he could then choose from. I began to strategically spread them all over the apartment to give Pete the hint that it was time to make a move. I thought it pretty ingenious to hide them inside his folded underwear and socks, work shirts, pants pockets, and his wallet. Looking back, I know that was not the avenue to take. I did, quite possibly, force Pete into a proposal.

> A wife is bound as long as her husband is alive. But if her husband should fall asleep in death, she is free to be married to whomever she wants, only in the Lord.
>
> —1 Corinthians 7:39

CHAPTER 19

That Fall, Pete proposed to me. It was not a great proposal. In fact, it was demeaning. Pete and I had a fight right before the holiday. It was not my finest hour. I was yelling about something, and he turned to me saying, "And to think I wanna marry you." Oh! My gosh! *Humiliating* is not a strong enough word. I recall walking right out of the bedroom and retreating to the front room. I was so taken aback. Not because he was going to ask and I messed it up, but because he decided to blurt that out in an argument.

Within a week, we went to the jewelry store together. I obviously knew why as I waited in the car. When Pete came out, he handed me the box; I opened it and that was it. I said, "I love this ring, it's so beautiful." It was gorgeous actually. I had to ask him if he was going to propose. Finally, he did. No, I never dreamed about my wedding proposal, but I certainly did not imagine it to have gone that way. Every girl expects fireworks. We want an imaginative one, a wonderfully memorable one. Perhaps my proposal was not that way, because Pete never really loved me. He could not, after all, tell me why he wanted to marry me. *Red flag!*

I immediately called my mom to share the news, but she was not home. I called Danny's wife, Suzette. She appeared to be so excited for us. I asked her to keep the engagement a secret and not to say anything to anyone. I really wanted my mom to hear it from me. Suzette, without me knowing, called my mom and Leslie when we had gotten off the phone. I was beyond livid with her for an extended time. It was never her place to do that. Another sizzled moment for me. When I finally got to share the news with my mom and Steve, the thrill was definitely gone. I still wore a big smile of gratitude. My mom was overjoyed for me. Knowing she was happy made me happy. But why *so* happy? Was I finally going to have a man take care of me?

Pete and I shared the news with the whole family that Christmas, at my grandma's home and Mrs. Abby's. Most of the family said it was about time. After six years of dating, it was time in my mind too. Know this though: Just because I thought it was time, does not mean it was the right time. When you have to tell someone to take such a major step without them initiating it themselves, it is not as rewarding. You can date someone for twenty years and yet have it still feel off. That is intuition.

January of 1994 was here. In addition to the other plans being made for the wedding, I had to choose who would perform the ceremony. Pete and I agreed there was only one person who would suffice, Fr. Stanley. Fr. Stanley, a Franciscan monk, was my grandpa's cousin. I quickly sent a letter off to him, requesting his presence at the wedding. He accepted in a letter that came from Rome, Italy. It was quite a blessing for Pete and myself. We loved Father Stanley deeply. He was a great man of the cloth.

The wedding was planned for mid-August. Pete and I made all the arrangements ourselves. We paid cash for everything prior to the big event, so it would be less worrisome after the honeymoon. That turned out to be an excellent move on our part. Pete and I agreed we would marry in my grade school Catholic church, and in turn, raise the children Lutheran, in his church. St. Louis the King was booked, and Father Bob, the head priest, was contacted for the rental of the space.

Leslie and I went out on three occasions to dress hunt. We had no luck though. I was working one day, cleaning a house in Clinton Township and stumbled upon a bridal shop. As soon as I finished for the day, I went into the store trying on several dresses. I narrowed my search to four gowns, and invited whomever wanted come with me to help with deciding upon a dress. I knew I was going to buy my dress at that particular shop. My mom quickly volunteered, which made me happy. That weekend, we both ventured out to look at the gowns I had chosen. There were two which really stood out, but I wanted another opinion. To my surprise, my mom also picked one that I had fallen in love with. Then she proceeded to do a very unexpected thing and paid for it! My mom never did anything big for me, aside from buying my senior class ring ten years earlier, while I was still in high school. I excitedly accepted her gift, and she bought the dress.

Planning a wedding is not an easy task. There are so many details that go into the finished product. It was a good thing for me to have been very organized and quite proficient at planning. Pete also had two nieces getting married within months of our date. I wanted my day to be unique, having a flair of both of our personalities. To me, that was not going to be difficult. I knew I was different anyway, and it was important for me to show my uniqueness. Pete and I did the planning completely on our own, without input. If we did get outside suggestions, we did discuss them together.

I cannot say I had cold feet; it was something bigger than that. I worried about Pete and my relationship a lot, wondering if we had what it took for lasting love. I remember talking to my Auntie Rose when I graduated high school. She seemed to have an excellent marriage with Uncle Joe. I asked Auntie Rose back then what was the most important thing about marriage. She never missed a beat, telling me "communication." I then thought, in the present moment, did Pete and I have that? We did not.

Over the years, there were quite a few secrets I kept to myself. I either believed it did not seem logical to share them, or I felt in doing so, it violated my privacy. I was then, as I am today, very big on privacy. Privacy is good; however, it is a horrible way to begin a married life. Secrets are never a good idea when you are going to invest in giving your life to someone. Pete and I never had strong communication skills. We never talked in detail about what we wanted in our lives or for the years to come. We both wanted children; that was the extent of any conversation. We did not even discuss our differences on child-rearing. Beginning a life with someone calls for big discussions to be had. I was learning all of those things hands-on; it was a huge challenge. After all, my family never communicated, unless through yelling, accusing, or scolding. I knew how to talk with people; however, I never learned how to fully listen, neither did Pete. *Red flag!*

Pete and I were complete opposites, which is how I thought it was supposed to be. I always heard, "Opposites attract." Yes, it is factual, although not practical. I know it happens all the time, but being compatible with one another is the ultimate goal. In my personal life, I have learned it is of the utmost importance to have a lot in common, with the person you pick as your partner. You have to know, in getting married, it is a decision for your lifetime. It is the person with whom you will give your better years too; they are the individual who will care for you as you age. Think about that for a moment...

Being with someone who longs to be in your company is an indication the person likes you. The like must come before the love. You cannot have love without liking someone first. It can be done, but it will never thrive, let alone survive. Pete and I were not friends; I think we both knew it. We were not friends, I believe, because we did not have a lot in common. If I knew all those things existed, prior to the marriage, it would have made sense to run. I had fear driving me though, the fear that no one could ever want me. How did that thought, and those feelings, come to be? It was a learned belief.

As our date approached, I still could not believe I was getting married. The excitement for the day overflowed within me. All the arrangements were going wonderfully well. I was getting the liquor for the reception, planning the menu for the caterers and having my wedding dress altered. My family was not assisting in any way. Leslie and Josie were off with their families. Even though Leslie lived a short distance from me, and I babysat constantly for her two little ones, she never offered a helping hand, other than to browse for dresses, a year earlier. I realized quite quickly she was envious of me and my upcoming wedding. She and Patrick had eloped. That was her choice, having a wedding was mine.

Everything was fast approaching. The only thing missing was Whitney. After all of our history, we did lose touch years prior. Elizabeth and I experienced a large amount of time away from each other, but we touched base again. She and I remained close, although not seeing each other often. We did not hang out much, because by now, Elizabeth was a single mom raising two daughters. Even though we did lose touch a few years earlier, she and I spoke often following the wedding. I admire her; she was and continues to be an excellent mom.

Elizabeth, although in my life, was not in the wedding party. I did not want to burden her with the money she needed to invest. I knew it was hard for her with work and raising her daughters. I needed to leave that decision to Elizabeth though. I never even asked her to stand up, and later had much regret about it. She was visibly hurt, and that was *never* my intention. I wanted to have had my oldest and dearest friend as my maid of honor. After all, the girls I had standing up in the wedding party were not girlfriends, only acquaintances. Today, I am not in contact with any of them.

I slept at my mom and Steve's the night before the wedding. All the out-of-town girls in the wedding party stayed with me. That included my two girlfriends from Knoxville, Rhoda, from the pet store, and Patty, Adam's sister. We had a blast that night, making it a point not to not stay up too late. The wedding was an afternoon ceremony; we had plenty of time to rest.

The morning of my special day, the flowers were delivered. Oh! My goodness! They were everything I had envisioned. Beautiful spring flowers colorfully surrounded by Monte Casino. They were stunning. One of my cleaning accounts owned a flower shop. Candy and I worked out a deal there was no cash exchanged. She did all of the arrangements for fifteen hundred dollars, and in lieu of paying her, I cleaned her home for six months. It was a terrific trade: the best I had made.

Steve and I sat down and chatted while the other girls got ready. The first thing he said was, "Are you nervous?" "No." I smiled. "Just scared." He chuckled and told me, "There's no reason, you're gonna look beautiful." That really was not what I had on my mind. I was authentically scared to get married and say, "yes". I wanted to be happy; but honestly, I wondered if I could be. I was twenty-seven years old. Getting married, to me, was a lifelong commitment. I thought in my mind, Once you take the plunge, that's it; you're in it for life, till death do you part.

Following breakfast, the bridesmaids, my mom, and I went to Lakeside Mall for our morning appointments. My mom paid for all of the bridesmaids to have makeup and up-dos done at JC Penney Salon. The bill had to have been close to eight hundred dollars, plus tips. That was so very generous, and I was beside myself. My mom insisted though. She said, "I didn't get to do this for your sisters. I'm doing it for you." Josie got married in Tennessee and borrowed a dress from a friend. We just showed up. Leslie wore street clothes to her ceremony when she eloped. No one was there to witness that union.

Back at my moms, all the girls and I put our dresses on and finished the final touches to our hair and makeup. Steve took my shoe off and dropped a penny in it. He said, "It's tradition, it's for good luck." I happily accepted. My dress was stunning. The bodice was all beaded, with a sweetheart neckline, and pinched sleeves made full bows at my shoulders.

My veil and headpiece were also beaded. I, for the first time since making my First Communion, felt beautiful. My grandma said so also, as soon as she saw me. Getting married and making a lifelong commitment is a large undertaking. It is not about the dress, reception, or menu. It is about love, understanding, and comradery.

When we arrived at the church, we made our way through the side doors, seeing Pete's driver circle the block until all the girls were inside. The flowers in the church were spectacular. The vases were huge in height, and the flowering blooms overtly colorful. Pete and I left them behind after our ceremony for the couple getting married following us. They made a definite addition to the altar. St. Louis the King, my school and church, since 1966, and now I was getting married here. The same place I made my Baptism, First Communion, Confirmation, and now Marriage.

For my wedding day, there where specific things I wanted, as would any bride. I wanted all of the flowers in the wedding party, church, and reception to be spring bouquets—they were! I wanted both my dad and Steve to walk me down the aisle—they did! I wanted to walk down the aisle to "Ave Maria" instead of the traditional wedding march—I did! I wanted my niece, Mary, to be my flower girl—she was! I wanted freshly carved prime rib at the reception—there was! (That was a special treat for Steve.) I even rode in a limousine for the first time. All those things were wants, not needs. God blessed me with each and every one of them. God brought Pete to me for a reason; I was clear on that.

Many of us were in the massive vestibule beforehand. It is where the girls stayed until it was time to walk down the aisle. Father Stanley came and joined us for a moment, praying over me. I was taken in by his huge heart and abundance of love. The ceremony was memorable, and everything went off without any real problems. The only thing I regretted was crying all the way down the aisle and never hearing "Ave Maria" being sung live. I wept for the entire walk, wearing a huge smile, while tears of joy rolled down my cheeks. I was overjoyed. My dad and Steve were on my arms. Pete looked so handsome, so debonair. I loved that moment in time. Pictures and a ride through the city while I stood out of the sunroof of the limo roof followed. I had many people honking, wishing us well. I was elated. Pete and I were married.

> If only my anguish could be fully weighed and
> put on scales together with my calamity.
>
> —Job 6:2

CHAPTER 20

It took less than three months for things to begin a subtle then forceful decline within our relationship. All the put-downs, insults, and snide comments became intensified as Pete metamorphosed into another personality. He was the same snide man; however, he was now verbally mean. I did not want to believe it all. It took me approximately six months into the marriage to confirm I had indeed married my mom. Yes. Pete had become a hard, tactless, verbally abusive racist. That was heartbreaking for me, even though I knew it years earlier. After getting married, I thought he was going to be my solace. It began, my journey of bad nightmares, which became a reality.

Pete's words became piercing daggers to my soul, heart, and mind. I was in shock and equally devastated. *Why is this happening?* was my thought. After contemplating the enormous life decision that I had just gone through, I realized God set the whole situation up. I was clear He had brought Pete and I together for a reason. What was it? Being that my mom was never there for me growing up, nor was she supportive, nor did she give me any type of validation, I was furious to be going through it again. I got married to have a better life than my upbringing. Now, it was all being repeated.

I prayed a lot during that time. My prayers were bold and descriptive once again, just as they were growing up. After all, I prayed for Pete and many of the traits he possessed, I figured God could assist me and direct me. I went to church, lit candles, and waited. I waited on God, but I was also proactive. I had always been that way; it was no time to change who I was. After all, I loved my personality. Pete and I were butting heads at every turn. Our egos were clashing, and I began to feel inadequate. I continued to pray and listen for guidance.

A year after getting married, Pete and I bought a home of our own. We were right down the street from Lac St. Clair. That was something enormous for a girl born to the east side of Detroit. I loved the parks, activity center, and library. The area was beautiful. Pete had grown up in the city and he took it all for granted, but everything was new to me. My first thought when seeing the city as a homeowner was *What a great place to raise a family*. Pete and I gutted and remodeled our home. Everything was fresh and new. We laid tiles, put a new bathroom in, and completely renovated the kitchen. I realized, Pete and I worked well together when I did what he wanted. That was not an equal union, and I was not that kind of person.

Pete and I talked about children before and after getting married; we both agreed we wanted to wait. We had two cats, a cockatiel, and a massive yard to tend to. Both of us had work to perform and our new house had to be made into a home. Having a baby was on the back burner for the time being, although we both knew we wanted to be parents one day. Paddy and Mara married in a chapel two years before Pete and I. They too lived in the same city, three blocks from our home.

Pete, Paddy, and Rick entered into a business venture together approximately two years after we married. Rick was just an investor; he had a corporate job. Pete and Paddy now owned and operated an auto mechanic repair shop and worked together every day all day, with the exception of Sunday. It was literally a dream come true for all three men. The twins had the life they had dreamed of, and I was so overjoyed for them.

I was working hard at my cleaning service. I still cleaned for Connie at the boat marina and had several commercial and residential accounts. I took on additional jobs, which was more sensible in paying household bills, and now a mortgage. We loved our home once we finished it. Pete and I now had a space that reflected both of our personalities. Together, we landscaped the front yard, and Pete built a garden in the back. I designed and created outdoor flower gardens throughout the backyard. I finished it off with a pussy willow tree, birdhouses, and rose bushes; everything was complete. The roses came from the old home in Detroit; they belonged to my Grandma Anita, my dad's mom.

Pete and I finally had it all together, and in the Fall of 1996, he surprised me with a thirtieth birthday party. It was hard to believe Pete and I had been together for ten years. Josie was even there, with Brenda; I was authentically surprised. I had never had my own birthday party growing up. Leslie and I shared ours, because our dates were two days apart from one another. I finally had my own cake, and it felt so right!

Things seemed to be going quite well, and Pete and I decided it was time to start a family. I became pregnant immediately. During my pregnancy, I put my ailing cat, Chloe, to sleep. Weeks later, my cockatiel, Chipper, passed away in his cage. I was so sad and lonely for many months. Everything was happening at once. I felt as if a part of me had died. Both animals were over twelve years old and they had wonderful lives. Knowing my heart would eventually bring me comfort, and perhaps God was preparing us. I had Chloe since working at the pet store in Knoxville. It was an emotionally trying time.

In the winter months of 1998, Pete and I were in the hospital, delivering our baby. I had meditative Yanni music playing while Pete assisted me with my breathing. He really did an excellent job during the delivery, never leaving me. We welcomed into the world, our baby girl, Melonie Joy. Not only was she perfect; she had my rare blood type. Melonie was part of me, undeniably. That single act was the most incredible thing to have ever happened to me in my life.

Melonie brought us so much joy. She was smart, articulate, and laughed constantly. At eleven months old, she mastered any kind of six-piece puzzle set and was cruising the furniture. I adored being with her so very much and still attempted to service my accounts. I went back to work and Lydia, my brother Henry's wife, was indispensable at caring for Melonie. That lasted only a few months before I realized I could not be productive while working. I was unable to concentrate on anything, except my new baby. After a long discussion of my telling Pete I had to stay home with Melonie, I officially became a stay-at-home mom. It turned out to be the best decision I could have made for my daughter. If we were to pay for a daycare, or a private babysitter for the week, there would be no substantial amount of money left. Plus, she would be with her mommy. I was elated at the idea of teaching my daughter everything she learned. We played, read, and danced all the time, listening to music and having ongoing teachable moments.

During my time of staying home, Elizabeth came by with her brand-new daughter, number 3 for her. It felt awesome to see her and catch up on the old and the new. We had connected a year earlier when she had gotten remarried. It was as though I had come full circle, leaving behind the abused little Barbara. Now I had a husband, a brand-new baby, and Elizabeth. Life was amazing; and I felt so blessed.

Melonie brought much happiness and many laughs into our home. Mrs. Abby and my mom were attentive grandmas. Papa Steve loved her cheeks. What a coincidence! Nothing, I thought, could change my happiness. Looking in Melonie's eyes brought me pure joy. I knew she was going to have that effect on me, so I gave her the middle name of Joy. My grandpa said that word all the time, showing gratitude to God. He now eternally lived through Melonie's name.

In the evenings, when I rocked my sweet baby to sleep, I asked God to keep her healthy and prayed for Melonie to have a great life. I know God still listened to me when I chatted with Him. I have faith that will never change. After all, He had never let me down before. Yes, I was subjected to a lot of abuse in my life; however, now I felt it was my time to prove my nurturing instincts were right on. It was crystal clear God was teaching me, but what exactly was the lesson?

I describe the next year as a roller coaster, because Pete was working all the time. He and Paddy began staying at the shop to continue repairing cars on more than an occasional Sunday. That made me furious. Sunday's were always busy with big dinners, home-time, and play. Paddy and Mara had a son too, Bradley. He was born a year before Melonie. I wondered if Mara minded Paddy's time away from home, like I minded it. Pete became distant and work was everything to him now.

By the end of 1998, we were struggling financial. Admittedly, I was spending a lot of money on Melonie, and I was not working. Not having the funds did not phase me though, and Melonie and I drove to see Josie and Brenda in Tennessee. Brenda was already in high school; she was a great help with the baby. Brenda bonded to Melonie, and they quickly became playmates. I needed to see Josie, although Pete could not understand why. Josie was a loving sister to me, and she and I did get along famously. There were, however, two sides to her personality. Pete did not understand why I subjected myself to that. If only he had stopped to see that he was the same way.

Pete and I were fighting a lot; I even packed Melonie up one evening, spending the night at my mom and Steve's. I would have liked to have gotten a hotel room, but there was no money for that. I was reduced to asking for help, something we were taught never to do. I was humiliated, totally humiliated. But in reality, I had nowhere to go. Steve and I conversed quite a bit that night while my mom and Melonie were playing and bonding.

I explained to Steve how Pete was treating me and how Pete was drinking all the time now. He told me to go back home in the morning and "make the best of it." I agreed to do that, obviously having no other alternative. I believed, because Steve was a recovered alcoholic, he may have had a talk with Pete. If he did, it fell on deaf ears. Pete treated me like he was doing me a favor by being with me. How could that be?

The disagreements were now a regular part of our days. Pete and I were not compatible on any level. I never felt listened to, and I believe my ideas were considered to be foolish. I did not feel loved or validated as a wife or mother. Even though I felt good about my mothering skills, others judged me. I reminded myself I was different than my mom, and how she raised me. I knew I would always be there for my children, unconditionally loving them. I do not believe it bothered me to actually be judged; I was bothered by others' thoughts that I was unable to be a great mom.

I came to the conclusion; Pete and I should get a certain book to read together. I purchased *Men Are from Mars, Women Are from Venus*, and we read it as a couple. It was an excellent source of information, and it gave a boost to our relationship. We even went so far as to highlight the pages where we mutually found helpful tips. It was wonderful to me; Pete and I had rekindled our romance. Simply reading the words another person felt was helpful information. Those words changed our perspective on viewing our differences. I felt in my heart Pete did not want to talk to me disrespectfully, just like I did not want to yell at him.

Sixth commandment: Thou shall not kill.
—Deuteronomy 5:17

CHAPTER 21

In June of 1999, I found out I was pregnant again. Pete was taken aback, to put it mildly, when I finally informed him. There were many negative comments to follow. Pete said, "Having another child will financially break us," "We can't afford the one we have now." I disagreed, knowing in my heart the baby was from God. I was happy; Melonie would have a playmate and friend to grow up with. Bradley never came around; Mara saw to that. Baby number 2 was not planned, but God always prevails.

Truth be told, I was so used to having two incomes and my own money. I had spent tons of cash on Melonie. I knew I had to go on a budget and was sure I could do it. I had never budgeted my money and was not sure how to do it. Since my mom never taught me, I thought Pete could instruct me. Instead, he assumed I would learn. How, and by whom though? I went to the library for more information. That was not helpful for me.

Pete and I were fighting so much in the evenings once Melonie was asleep. I hated being told what to do, or even worse, being told what I could not do. Pete felt he could begin putting restrictions on me, and then assumed my habits would change immediately. I felt it insurmountable for me to achieve *all* those things he was demanding in a quick manner. I did, after all, have to create a budget and stick to. I vowed not to spend money on Melonie unless it was a necessity. That meant purchasing training pants, toiletries, and food only. I thought, *I could do all of these things*. I knew I needed at least a month.

Pete was a great saver, but I was not taught that. It proved to be another opposing personality trait. The truth was, Pete knew I could not manage money; he knew it coming into the relationship. I exceeded a month before getting my spending under control. *Pete expects so much from me*, I thought. I felt I was deliberately being set up for a fall. I had tons of stress to contend with. The second time around of being pregnant was rough on my mind and body. It was nothing like Melonie; her pregnancy was easy-flowing.

I had a lot of morning, afternoon, and evening sickness carrying baby number 2. I was exhausted all the time yet played with Melonie constantly. My body did not seem the same, putting aside the fact I was with child. I prayed repeatedly asking God to make me healthier. I never seemed to get enough rest. The stresses continued to pile up on me, and being pregnant took an enormous toll on my body. Nothing I did appeased Pete. He was becoming a constant thorn in my heart and began trying to manipulate my thinking. I repeatedly let him know how his words maimed me, stabbing me like a dagger. He seemed to care less and less about me. That became hard to swallow. I found, by tracking my moods, I was depressed at night but fine during the day. That is when I was busy with Melonie. Those feelings stayed with me, not dissipating in the least.

On a cold Michigan afternoon, at the start of the millennium, my sweet little Adaline was born. She too, like Melonie, was perfect in every way. Now, both of my daughters shared my rare blood type. Adaline had a full head of brown hair, my color. Melonie was a blonde with blue eyes, and was an equal image of her daddy. Many more visitors were there for Adaline. I suppose I had loosened up, allowing additional people to visit the second time around.

Having two babies was exciting. I had to do a lot of planning now. There was extra cooking and lots of cleaning, but I enjoyed it all. Pete and I had a family. We were a unit, created by the two of us. Wow! It was an amazing feeling. We dressed the girls alike for fun, and I constantly did arts and crafts with them. As soon as Adaline could hold her spoon, she held a crayon. Melonie loved Adaline. They always played alongside and with each other.

I began feeling tired and run-down, even a bit melancholy. Despite the fact that it was fun, things became hard. Being a stay-at-home mom, cooking, cleaning, banking, and all the other responsibilities became overwhelming. *Surely I need a vacation or a long rest*, I thought. I had never felt that way before. Those feelings became constant and harder to push away. They continued for three months, eventually making me feel utterly depressed and hopeless. Those are two feelings you cannot have when being a productive mom. I made an appointment with my family doctor for the following week.

I believed I was showing symptoms of postpartum depression, after doing some reading and talking with my mom. I discussed my emotions at length with Dr. Finkelstein, and he prescribed an antidepressant for me. I will tell you, it is not a joke being depressed. The new drug prescribed in a two-week period of time sent me skyrocketing with agitation and confusion. I spiraled into a deep depression. I had to give the medication time to work, but after the trial, I knew it was not the one for me. The process continued until June of 2000, trying medication after medication. An additional four months would crawl by, and I did not feel any relief. My head felt as if it would explode at any given moment. My eyes were swollen in pain; my heart pounded with anxiety. I could not figure out why I felt so differently now that Adaline was here.

I prayed so much, asking God to help me. I was trying to take care of my girls, but longed to die. These two little children were all I thought about. I found hope in that. Hope was given to me by God. I had a reason to live, and it was my daughters. They continued to keep my mind somewhat steady as I made it through the days that passed. I listened intently for God. He directed me to the library one day. Upon walking in, I had no idea where I was going. I knew I wanted the mental health section but had no clue where it was. I stood in the middle of the library in stillness and listened. I learned a bit about meditation, and it worked for me. So, there I stood, for what seemed like ten minutes.

I never had a reason to visit the adult section of the library before. Truth be told, I was only a frequent visitor in the children's area those days. But God, He had bigger plans for me. I walked to the adult section and went to a specific area of books. I had no idea what I was doing consciously, but my steps were that of knowing. I picked a book off the shelf. It was a title depicting different mental illnesses. I kept listening to my mind, though, as it repeatedly said, *I have to look up paranoid schizophrenia.* I opened the book to a specific page, thinking the whole time that I should be looking in the index. I wanted to do what was in my mind, not in the unknowing.

When I looked down at the page, I had opened in the first book I had picked up, it had a description of Bipolar I on one side, Bipolar II on the other. I was instantly confused as I had never heard of the illness, but I began to peruse the page. I then read the term "Manic Depression," and that name I was familiar with. I attentively read both pages in detail. Having felt the tug to check the book out, I immediately showed it to Pete once I returned home. "Is that how you feel?" There was a huge question mark in his voice. "Yes," I said.

I made a quick appointment with Dr. Finkelstein, and I had my library book in tote. We discussed the contents of what was read and he said, "No, this isn't you at all." "Yes, it really is," I refuted. Looking up from the corner of his eyes, he sadly and simply commented, "This is beyond my field of expertise. You will go to St. Joseph's for an evaluation." My first thought—my very first thought—was, *During all the turmoil in my life, I am forever surrounded by saints*. Then, in my mind, all hell broke loose. I mean hell. I was happy and sad multiple times a day. My mind was tired, but I had two little girls to take care of. Adaline was not even walking yet.

The same day, after my doctor's appointment, I made an immediate trip to St. Joe's for an intake and examination. They diagnosed me as having Bipolar I. The news was a blow to me. I was sure it was Bipolar II, the lesser of the two. I was devastated. I felt certain it was a death sentence. My dad was sick all of his adult life; was that what was going to happen to me? I drove home in disarray thinking, *What's my family gonna say?* I knew I would not get support. I thought I may, but in my heart, I knew I would not. In looking back, I realized my family made me reliant upon them. That makes me sick today—the knowledge that a family, an entire family, *used* me.

I was happy to have a name to describe how I felt. God was listening to my prayers every time I asked for help. God, as I was always told, helps those who help themselves. I was! Pete felt...well, I am not sure how he felt. He never discussed it. Actually, Pete never discussed anything, except money. There were many things I wanted to talk with him about. There were several words that I never got to speak. I did begin to feel like a leopard around those very individuals whom I thought loved me unconditionally. Pete included.

I never received encouragement from Pete, my mom, or my born-into family. It was a time; however, I expected everyone to pull together as a family should, to be there emotionally for me. I needed unconditional love, understanding, and patience with my new diagnosis. Looking back, I should not have expected any of that. It really was not logical after all. I was the black sheep of the bunch since the time I was born. I was still fending for my own soul at thirty-three years old. My thoughts drifted and I asked God, *Why would I be alone my entire life in this way? What lessons am I to learn from this?*

Being regulated for the correct medications became another battle for my mind. There was a short amount of time; I felt remarkable thinking the medications were working. Then I crashed again, falling into a fiery pit of depression. I always took care of myself; now was no different, so I believed. Sometimes when you are down to the lowest depths possible, it is up to you and only you to pull yourself out. Many times, it is the only way to save yourself. For me, that moment was here. I also did everything the doctors said. I was not doing any drinking because I was breastfeeding Adaline. So, I began to eat properly and exercise again. I regularly hooked two umbrella strollers together. Then the girls and I would get fresh air walking through the neighborhood. Sometimes we went to the park. That truly helped me. When depression hits, exercise and routine are so important for one's psyche.

Now who is there to harm you if you are zealous for what is good?
—1 Peter 3:13

CHAPTER 22

During the battle in my mind, I went to visit my dad, telling him everything I was going through. I felt he could help me come to terms with the diagnosis. The only thing my father suggested was to "Keep it to yourself, daughter." Well, he apparently did not know me. I believe my dad was referring to the backlash from ignorance. He was right on. I found out, quite quickly, the stigma toward mental illness was still very much alive. Ignorance was not it, but instead it was *fear*. I grew to realize people feared what they did not know. *Why not educate yourselves?* were my thoughts.

I stayed with the first doctor for a year after I began treatment. Celia Lake, my original intake therapist at St. Joe's, was part of my medical team for many years to follow. She went on to be the first therapist to ever validate my feelings. I finally found the right medications for my illnesses, and my pharmaceutical regiment got less complicated. I did not like taking all the medications, but I had no choice. I learned early on to never miss a dosage. If I had, my meds became less effective. I was finally feeling decent, and I obviously did not want to relapse.

I began therapy again, and Pete was very attentive for a month or so. He helped immensely with Melonie and Adaline. Pete cleaned, cooked, did laundry, even helped put the girls to bed when I needed assistance. I knew he saw the strain in my eyes because he did help. I *was* his wife, in sickness and in health. However, soon Pete did not want to believe my illness was indeed real. Many things changed.

Pete and I went periods of time without sex and that hurt me a lot. I wanted to be with him, but mentally, I could not. He did prove, on more than one occasion, he was only interested in my getting better. That did not last though. Soon it became apparent, sex was all that would make Pete nice. I thought, after agreeing several times to it, I most certainly could not be with a negative person any longer. I was constantly belittled and put down. The distance grew between us both. I rejected wanting to be with Pete, simply because of his personality and the way in which he verbally abused me.

I often suggested to Pete to go out with Paddy. I felt it was the healthy thing for him to do for himself. I knew how drained I was, being at home working, but Pete worked physically harder. It was a lot to handle. I tried to make things go smoothly for the household. I always had dinner prepared at the end of the day, and the girls and I made crafts for Daddy. Pete appreciated that, and the fact my medications were working. I was bound and determined to be the mom I never had and the wife my mom never was. I was inspired by being a mom to Melonie and Adaline, and they were my motivation.

My girls and I had much enjoyment with one another. We played at the park, took trips to the library and zoo, and drove long distance to visit Josie and Brenda. We did everything together. I loved my baby girls so much. I could not imagine ever being away from them, but I knew my batteries were wearing down. I was moving ever so slowly, going to bed earlier, and sleeping ten to twelve hours a night. Then, before too long, the putdowns started creeping in again. I was not acting irrationally, but Pete commented to me, "Your meds must not be working." The fact was my medications were working very well. That was the time the verbal degradation began, and Pete introduced the girls into his twisted way of thinking.

The insults made everything more difficult. Everything! My mind spun, my head throbbed, and my mouth flapped. I was slowly learning self-worth in therapy. Up to that point in my life, I let people degrade me when they made me feel unintelligent; I usually did not comment. I truly had enough of it, and could not comprehend allowing that torture to continue. Pete put me down continuously, but I refused to take it any longer. I verbally gave him a piece of my mind, and he in change, verbally humiliated me. It was never an equal playing field. My delivery may have come in the form of yelling; however, I never put Pete's manhood down. He was coming at me with years of resentment spewing from his mouth. Pete also insulted my father and myself, all the while smiling and laughing out, "You're both screwed in the head."

I was still seeing Ms. Lake, my therapist. It was now going on two years since I was first diagnosed at St. Joe's. I was extremely honest with Celia, explaining how I was going crazy being around Pete. He was harassing me constantly with crude remarks. I never got why he felt the need to treat me that way. Was it that he resented me for getting sick? I explained to Celia how I needed a break, some time away. Pete was threatened with my illness because he refused to educate himself in what my diagnosis was.

Pete could not throw me into a hospital for long-term care since I was sane. I worried about that daily. He was doing things, malicious things behind my back. Pete was chatting with my family quite a bit too. That in itself was terrifying. I just had bipolar, a very treatable form of mental illness. Many things were different from when my dad was sick, and basically that was my comparison for myself. The main difference was I was a functioning adult. My dad had a mental breakdown and never recovered. My mom dropped my dad like a hot potato. Pete did not do that, though; he was staying by my side. I often wondered why, since he treated me and spoke to me so rudely. I realized he had a lot of anger in him. *Red flag!* Now I needed to find out the connection to me. Why had I married a man who treated me like my family did? That question would be answered, but not until several years later.

Celia and I discussed my need to get away, repeatedly. I felt it quite possible for me to end up having a nervous breakdown, or worse taking my life. I needed a break. Celia asked me during many therapy sessions if I was coherent and aware of what I was doing. I told her, "Without any doubt, I'm all here." I never lied to my therapists. After all, I was there to get help. I did not care if they judged me silently; I wanted to pick their brains for ideas and information. I wanted concrete remedies for betterment. Since my medications had me stable, I knew what was going on around me on many levels. My suspicions of Pete grew stronger.

I, being very detailed, planned a trip. I felt an overwhelming need to save and attempt to heal my own psyche. I knew if I did not do something, I was going to, at minimum, end up in the hospital. I would be absolutely no help to my daughters then. Even though I was treated poorly, I saw what a great job Pete did taking care of our girls. That proved to be another naive moment for me.

I made reservations for Nassau, Bahamas, leaving a couple of weeks afterward. When I told Pete I needed to get away, I told him I was going to Florida. That was the only lie. I gave him all the other information, such as departure and landing times. I could not stay. I had to get away, far away, and leave for a bit of time. I set up babysitters in advance for the week, my mom and Mrs. Abby. I made sure to have the house cleaned, food cooked then frozen, and the laundry was completed. I explained to both ladies I was taking a small vacation in lieu of my having been sick. I let my mom and Steve know where I was going though. My mom seemed supportive at the time.

I had no remorse getting on the plane. That may sound really bad; however, I believe I was given a *heads-up* by God. If I had not gone on that trip, I know today I would be dead. I would have killed myself because my mind was being sucked empty by Pete. It was yet another moment where God was directing me to take care of myself. No, God did not say "Go to the Bahamas," but He did nudge me to save myself before it became too late.

I went to the Bahamas with an exhausted mind. *I would be refreshed and ready to begin life again once I returned.* That was my plan. My first day on the island was so relaxing. I went to an outdoor barbecue where there was live music, many bohemian people, and a lot of dancing. I was a social butterfly, although I had not felt that way in a very long time. I mingled upon arriving and met three wonderful locals who took me under their wings. We went to a few different clubs to dance that night. It was an amazing experience, and I felt like Barb again. I was in the heat and sunshine. The vitamin D was a much-needed supplement, one which I had been deficient in for a long time. I was meeting people and having adult conversations. I felt great, and the revitalization was beginning to happen.

Three days into my week, I called home to check on everyone. Pete was screaming at me over the phone, "No wonder your phone won't work; you're in another country." After I pulled my stomach off the floor, I calmly explained to him why I was there of all places. Pete evidently got on the computer and went through my history. He found out after calling the travel agency, I was in Nassau, not Florida. Pete did not hear anything I said. He just continued insulting me. Even though I had taken a trip to get away from his mouth, here he was screaming at me, yet again.

I went back to the hotel room, called Celia, and had an hour-long conversation with her. She told me Pete had been calling her office all week, yelling and swearing vulgarities on his messages. I was so embarrassed, even though I knew Celia had heard it all before. She said something to me that switched the whole game up. She asked me, "Do you think going away was a mistake?" I quickly answered, "No way." She then said, "You're there already, and you can't change that. Have as much fun as you can before you have to come back." That was solid, great advice!

The next day, I took a tour around the entire island with my new friend and guide, Leo. It was so beautiful and peaceful. I took every bit of the surroundings in, even stopping at a native bohemian restaurant. I bought Melonie and Adaline hand-crocheted matching outfits and took in all the sights of the town. I took advantage of my time alone, and I meditated on the beach, facing the vast ocean. I even had my hair braided by a local lady and ate conk salad every day. I loved the island so much; I envisioned retiring there. The calm, hot, and easygoing atmosphere was what I longed for and absolutely what I needed.

> Even if my own father and mother abandon
> me, God himself will take me in.
>
> —Proverbs 1:7

CHAPTER 23

Returning home was a nightmare, a total living nightmare! Pete, my mom, Leslie, and Danny tore me up emotionally and mentally, and they verbally assaulted me. My mom, I learned, was a lying hypocrite. She knew I was going to the Bahamas; I told her and Steve everything. My mom sabotaged me, acting as if she knew nothing. Pete was accusing me of being a bad mother; I was not. He was attacking every string of my being. At that moment, with every essence of my soul, I hated him. He did not stop ripping me apart. I left to get relief from him in the first place. At that point, I knew Pete did not love me in any way. Now I had to figure out what I was going to do about that.

The following months proved to be unbearably difficult for me. I believe I had some kind of lapse in reasoning, because I stayed in the relationship. Pete treated me like hired help, literally. I was forbidden to spend any money, go anywhere that required money, and he was very adamant about my not working. He did not want me to seek employment, yet he constantly complained about not having any cash. Pete was full of double standards. I knew it was time to get a job.

I found a local hotel hiring for a desk clerk. I went to get the job, and I was hired immediately. I was now employed at an establishment, much more upscale than the hotels I was used to working at. Pete was happy when I got home and told him. I explained it was an afternoon position. That worked out well. Pete stayed home at night, and I was there during the day. Doing it that way allowed both girls to be with their parents, and we did not need daycare. With the money I made, I decided I to pay off my charge card. It was my responsibility I knew, so I planned on taking care of it. Little did I know Pete began insulting me behind my back, to my daughters.

I thought my decision to pay off the credit cards would make Pete happy; it did not. He was not, as I realized, a flexible person. Instead of my paying off the charge card, he wanted to be able to degrade me as much as possible for having taken the trip. That was not a fictitious thought; it was the reality I was living. If I paid my charge off, Pete had no reason to yell at me. That is not true though. He would then complain that I had spent my earnings on a credit card payoff—a debt that was not reasonable or necessary to begin with. Pete also said the bills could have been avoided if I had not been selfish. I was forever in a lose-lose situation with him.

I loved my new job and felt like a functioning adult again. My medications were working very well, and now I was being productive outside the home. There is no feeling comparable to working and bring money home. I had gotten over how I was treated when I came back from my trip. I had Melonie and Adaline to raise; there was no time to carry grudges, so I did not. I felt God wanted me to rise up and be a better person. I had peace from within for having done it for myself. Instead of spending all of my earnings paying off the trip, I in reality needed to be saving half of my money for a rainy day. It was potentially another secret though, and I was afraid to do it. That proved to be a huge mistake on my part.

I found, in staying busy, it actually helped my bipolar symptoms. I had much more energy and was not sleeping long hours any longer. My schedule had become set, and I excelled. I now got home at eleven thirty, and I was awakening by six in the morning. I felt great physically and mentally other than being put down and belittled. I knew at that point it was going to be a way of life, and it was. Pete could not complain about things not getting done. I accomplished all of my tasks and even began the flowerbeds in the yard.

I had surrounded myself with good people whom I could count on in a pinch, so I thought. Elizabeth and Whitney were not in my life at the time. I did have a girlfriend, Carmen. She and I were not as close as my other friends. We met each other at our children's preschool, and her husband and Pete hit it off very well. We had dinner parties together, and the children got along together in a playful manner. I did not, however, confide in Carmen about my illness or other personal issues. Before long, though, she found out I had bipolar.

Danny and Suzette's youngest daughter made her First Communion, and we attended it as a family. It was a lovely Mass, but a horrible luncheon. I, while eating, had an anxiety attack. It came out of the blue. I nudged Pete, and we quietly excused ourselves from the table, going outside for air. I was fairly new with the illness, and I had not learned to fight off those attacks yet. It had only been two years having been diagnosed. I thought I was handling it, but in the thick of an attack, you should not be so preoccupied with *why*. Calming, friendly voices or music usually helped me. What was about to unfold was the complete opposite. I found out what many of my triggers were that day.

As I sat on the banquet hall's front porch, trying to breathe and catch my bearings, Leslie came out to sit next to me. She put her arm around my back, asking what had set it all in motion. I could not talk. She then began slapping me on the back hard, then harder. "Snap out of it," she kept insisting. I was so livid and flustered, I shoved her off of me, still not being able to catch my breath. After she went inside, I asked Pete what she came out for. I was fuming. I had not seen her in a year since a large verbal fall-out. She knew nothing about me or my life. Pete sat with me, attempting to calm me down.

That night, Pete let Leslie take Melonie and Adaline home with her. He thought it was going to help me calm down. Pete thought the girls should not see me in that manner. All it did was create more anxiety. Pete did that for other reasons. Those reasons I never found out about until years later. Not only did I not trust Leslie; I felt she was a bad mom. Why on earth would I leave my daughters with her? I could not in my heart.

I had not spoken to nor had I seen Leslie in over a year. Why did Pete think the solution was to have her take my daughters? She was not a good person in my eyes. I did not want her around my children. The year prior to that, she let Melonie drive alone in a car with someone I did not even know and without a car seat. When I called Leslie out on it, she said I was over-reacting. Well, that I believed, was my prerogative as a parent. Leslie was obviously not over the previous year's issue. The next day, at 8:30 in the morning, she brought Melonie and Adaline back home. My girls were two and four years of age. They came out of Leslie's car chewing gum. That was something I did not allow yet, and Leslie knew it. I told them to spit it out, and they did. I got them situated in the house when I noticed Leslie standing on my porch, peering through the picture window. I asked her to leave, telling her she was not welcomed back to our home, ever again!

Leslie became enraged. I never saw that side of her—never. She stood on my front porch, berating me. She said, "How is it that you get to go to the Bahamas and I can't?" I told her it was called credit cards. She was screaming at me and calling me all kinds of viciously degrading names. Leslie told me I was a bad mother and "very selfish." I realized immediately that she, for whatever reason, was seriously envious of me. I just kept laughing at her. I told her the situation was absolutely none of her business. She became so angry her eyes were bloodshot, and she was literally foaming at her mouth, looking like a ravaged dog. I again told her to "leave and never come back." She got into her car and sped away.

Carmen had asked me to watch her two children that particular morning. I had already made the plans a week earlier. John and Julie were great kids, and I could never turn them away. Carmen dropped her children off at nine thirty. By the time Carmen arrived, I was already calm but still upset over the situation. I explained to her what had happened. Carmen asked if I still wanted to watch her two children. "Without any doubt," I said. The four kids played together, and we all had a snack. When Carmen came at 11:45, she and I talked for a bit before she left.

At 12:15, Melonie and Adaline were watching TV, eating their lunches. There was a knock on the front door while I was on the phone. I asked Melonie to see who it was. Melonie pulled the blinds apart, saying, "It's Grandma B." "Let her in," I said. Once Melonie opened the door, I saw with my own two eyes. Leslie was hiding herself between my mom and Steve. All went chaotic! I hung the phone up immediately. I distinctly recall telling her to never come back again, yet here she was, disguising herself.

Leslie grabbed ahold of me, my mom in tow. Leslie put my hands behind my back, saying, "We're here to do an intervention." "The hell you are!" I yelled. She tried tackling me while pinning me against my kitchen counter, with her arms around my neck and chest. I bit her hand so hard, I felt my teeth touch top to bottom. I grabbed Leslie by the hair, taking her down to the floor. I did beat on her pretty well. I did not want my mom getting hurt, so I nudged her toward the refrigerator. I proceeded to finish trying to get Leslie off of me. She was not letting up, so I took her down to the tiled floor. I had no choice but to defend myself. It was me or her, and I was not going down that way, not in my own home.

My mom called the police and told them I was "erratic" and that I had just "assaulted" her. Yes, I was erratic; I was being played by my family. However, assault my mother? Never. I got on the phone with Celia immediately. She kept saying, "I need you to calm down," but I was unable to. Then Leslie screamed, "We're taking your kids. Where you're going, you won't be seeing them again." Leslie, I later found out, had told the cops I was "suicidal." Really? I had not had contact with Leslie in a long while. She did not even know my character. I surmised Leslie did a little one-on-one with *her* therapist. I was right. I found out Dr. Michelina suggested the intervention. He versed Leslie on the state laws in Michigan regarding the "mentally ill." Anyone can be held against their will for a three-day observation hold, if someone says they are suicidal. The cops will just take you to a hospital. So apparently, all Leslie had to do was lie. Now here I was, smack-dab in the middle of a huge misunderstanding.

I tried explaining to the police what happened, how they came into my home for an intervention. They did not listen to me, instead I was pepper-sprayed in front of my daughters. When the officer cleaned my eyes out some fifteen minutes later, Leslie was on my back porch, waving and smiling at me through the window. I went crazy with anger. I was put on a gurney, handcuffed, and taken to a hospital. I was humiliated by my family again. I thought to myself, *Why is Pete working? He should be here protecting me.* All of that transpired because I had been diagnosed with Bipolar I, and my family was fearful over something they refused to seek help for themselves. That was extremely close-minded and ignorant thinking on their parts.

During the time of observation, I did a lot of reflecting. I called Carmen to come be a witness to confirm my story that I had been fine in the morning. She did. At the time, I assumed Pete was in on the so-called "intervention." For the record, interventions are usually preformed with a psychologist in their office or another safe place. That was no intervention; it was Leslie getting back at me, pure and simple. I was being held at the hospital and was handcuffed the entire day and night. No one gave me any food, water, or information. Those officers believed Leslie's story about my being suicidal.

Pete finally showed up at the hospital late that afternoon. He acted surprised at what had occurred, but in my heart, I knew…Pete had more to do with what happened to me than he was telling. In my investigation of the whole situation, I found out Pete went to see Leslie's therapist, Dr. Michelina, when I was in the Bahamas. That "professional" told Pete and Leslie to do the intervention. He had never seen me, let alone evaluate me. Yet the man was able to give his "professional advice." I was visibly upset. That stranger did not know me! He never spoke with me but felt I needed an intervention. There are always three sides to the story. His, hers, and the truth.

The following morning, I got into an ambulance and was driven to another county. There were no available beds in my area. That was, as I found out, the best place I could have gone. In the midst of all the chaos, God was still in control; I just did not see it yet. God was orchestrating the entire situation; immediately after, Leslie did that awful thing to me. The ambulance drivers offered me a donut, telling me, "You don't seem crazy to us." I laughed telling them, "There's nothing wrong with me; it's my sister who should be in here."

Upon arriving to the locked-down unit at St. Joe's Oakland, I could not help but notice the bars on the windows. I thought I was going away for a long time. I was told the unit was for suicidal and homicidal people, from the gentleman checking me in. I began to have an anxiety attack, crying uncontrollably. Then an empathetic and knowledgeable nurse explained everything to me in great detail. I signed myself in to sign myself out three days later. Yes. I went through a psychological evaluation, saw a psychiatrist, and went to a group session. The nurse asked immediately, "Why are you here?" I explained I had Bipolar I, and my family did not accept it, so that is how they handled it. He asked if I was suicidal. "No" was my honest response. That male nurse changed my entire perception of the illness.

Nurse Matt asked me what I do to show I have bipolar. I said, "Well, I spend a lot of money I don't have." He explained that was *one* part of my illness. He confided in me, telling me how his grandmother had the illness too. For the following three days, Nurse Matt schooled me. I felt so much better when I left the hospital. I had a new lease on my sickness, and it was not the attitude of a defeated person. Three days later, Pete picked me up, and I went home. Nothing was ever the same. I never trusted nor believed in Pete again. I had an epiphany that day. I should have started saving money while I was working at the hotel.

The day following my release, Danny showed up at Pete and my home. Pete stood outside on the cobblestone walk, getting in Danny's face. They were screaming loudly. Adaline and I were in the front room drawing and coloring at the girl's table. Adaline drew a picture of Danny screaming. I felt helpless. I heard Danny tell Pete, "Why don't you take that psycho on your boat, tie your anchor to her, and drop that deadweight overboard?" When I heard that, I started crying; I felt the hate of all of my family, except for Henry and John. Why, though, did my family do that to me? They were far from being done too.

The only reason Danny felt that way was because of his sexual abuse against me. I know Danny knew it was going to eventually come out. But he wanted to do everything he could to make me look unstable. He should not have said what he did to Pete. Danny never liked me, that was why he molested me and tried to drowned me. I am *very* clear on that today. Maybe he thought I was going to tell on him because I was a "psycho bitch!" Pete kicked Danny off the property that day, telling him to never come to our home again. Pete was not sincere to me though. It was, after all, the same man who called me "a crazy bitch" and told me "You're just like your dad." I was not believing him.

Additionally, I was informed by the hotel I worked for that I no longer had a position there. That happened when Danny's wife, Suzette, called them. She informed them I was "psychotic and in the hospital." I was boiling over with anger. She had no place doing that. I went to Suzette and Danny's house, screaming up the driveway. "Come outside, child molester" is what I repeated over and over, telling Suzette what he did to me. I continued till Suzette closed the windows and doors, calling me a liar. If she only knew. Pete was in his truck, behind my car, telling me to "leave it alone." Pete did believe me when I told him about Danny's abuse. That meant something to me on a deep level. But, for the life of me, I did not know what. I left Danny's house that day, never to return again.

I found myself trying to defend my very being, just like I did as a young girl. That is an extremely uncomfortable place to be. You know in your heart who you are, but those closest to you are degrading and belittling you, simply because you are ill. I tried so vigilantly to grasp ahold of Bipolar. It is very difficult to help yourself when there are many facets to your functioning brain, competing for equality. I felt my family wanted me dead.

Around the same time, a paper was sent home from the children's school. It outlined in detail how a suspicious white van was seen around the school grounds. I became scared and was beside myself with added anxiety. I flashed back to Danny and the molestation he perpetrated against me. I became afraid to let the girls play out in front, and I took guard over them. Playing outside was a normal part of childhood they were now being deprived of. Thoughts and feelings for the need to protect my children became overwhelmingly strong, as they were both only in grade school.

I found myself at Steve and my mom's, telling them how Danny molested me growing up. My mom looked me straight in the eyes saying, "You liar, you're only saying that for attention." By now, Steve was at the door, and I was dressing the girls in their coats. I told my mom to take a good long look at her granddaughters because she would never see them again. Melonie, Adaline, and I left, never returning to their home again.

Put away from yourselves every kind of malicious bitterness, anger, wrath, screaming and abusive speech, as well as everything injurious. But become kind to one another, tenderly compassionate, freely forgiving another just as God also by Christ freely forgave you.
—Ephesians 4:31–32

CHAPTER 24

These were unbearably hard times for me, emotionally and moreover mentally. I no longer had a family to love me. The fact was, they never did. I now had to deal with that in the present moment. All those times my mom said, "I love you a bushel and a peck," was she lying? But why? Perhaps she was trying to convince herself. I believe my family was filled with secrets and shortcomings, and I was a mistake to my mom but a blessing to God. I loved Him, as my Father, wholeheartedly. Even though I knew that in my mind, I remained very depressed, knowing the illness had taken over me. Coming back from the brink proved to be a large undertaking; however, I did not think it was insurmountable.

I decided to go to our church, where Pete and I had been members since getting married. I felt I needed encouragement and some solid advice. Upon arriving, I had a conversation with the pastor, explaining my diagnosis. The moment I asked for Pastor Flaunt's help and guidance, he replied, with his hand on my shoulder, "You know, it's all in your head?" *What?* "That's a lie," I snarled at him as I stormed away. I never attended another service in that church. I felt if Pastor Flaunt believed that, even with his wife being an RN, he most definitely was not fit to be in charge of my religious needs. I left, devastated and torn. One single man blocked me from feeling the love of the church. I had been a Sunday school teacher there after all; I could not believe he treated me so coldly. Another ignorant, ill-informed person!

Not having the support of my church proved to have a devastating blow to my heart and mind. I believed God was working to find a new congregation for me, if I needed that. Until then, I prayed alone. I often found myself sitting in the cellar of the basement in our home. With the light off, I would cry in the dark. It was a safe place for me to have quiet in my head; it was a way for me to pray in peace. I before long realized I was comforting myself. I was finding an alone spot where I could retreat, just like I did as a young girl. I cried while talking to God, asking Him for overt signs. I prayed boldly for a way out of the madness. The madness, both in and out of my mind. When you do that, be prepared for what God asks of you. Do not question it if you know it is directly from Him.

I was alone in every aspect. I felt ugly, defective, and unwanted. I was a girl without a family, husband, or church. Thoughts of anguish, defeat, and unworthiness permeated my mind. I prayed hard for God to delivery me to my freedom. I needed to escape the hell I was in, but I had no clue how to do this. I felt as though my head was going to explode. I had numerous panic and anxiety attacks following the hospitalization. Everything I felt was personified by my environment. During that time, I dropped the friends I had and made new ones. I now chose people who built me up, ultimately helping me feel better about myself. I surrounded myself with people smarter than myself.

I began reading the few pamphlets that were available to me from various sources. I researched bipolar and read every book I took out from the library. God and I chatted. He told me I had to do for myself, and then He showed me what to do in becoming proactive. I listened to every word, becoming well-versed on my illness. I also did some internet searches based on information I needed or received. The information I found changed my opinions about others' perception of the illness. In many ways, it also changed mine.

I came across a webpage, sharing a different perspective and philosophy on illness. I became enthralled in being on line every time I had an available moment. The groups and people helped me to see I was not alone. I enjoyed that aspect as there were no "sit-in" groups on bipolar in my area. I did, for years to follow, continue to be a part of their bipolar support group.

I met fascinating individuals whom I believe were sent from God. One person in particular, Boz, became my confidant. He and I shared several conversations over the course of many months. Boz gave me alternative views on my illness, based on his experiences. He was, as I learned, an angel from God. He did not suffer any mental illness but was a doctor, advocate and facilitator, fighting for other individuals' recovery. He taught me to accept, learn, grow, and pass it all on. I became proficient at those concepts over time. It proved to be just what I needed.

Boz's role, I noticed, was to comfort and show genuine care. He explained to me how I was here for a bigger purpose. I shared everything with this stranger, who was years wiser than I. He had knowledge and experience with mental illness, and I had only read about recovery from bipolar. I confided in him of what my demons were, and he helped me see my worth. Boz never wavered from being my friend. I told him about Pete's treatment of me and my mind. I received real advice from Boz, not fake pats on my back, telling me it was all okay. No, Boz encouraged me, and I took every bit of his advice. It sounded sensible and I had been praying for information. I felt I had nothing to lose by trying his suggestions.

Melonie and Adaline were affected, there was no doubt. The yelling, screaming, and swearing from both Pete and myself was real in our home. I tried specifically being there for them but failed several times. My mind focused on them during the days when we were alone to learn and play. At night, when I was making dinner and after Pete got home, all hell engulfed me. They saw Mommy lose it many times because of the way Pete talked and responded to me. I often flew off the handle in response to something he said. The verbal abuse was overwhelming, and I felt Pete had it out for me merely by the way he spoke to me. Loving someone should never feel like torture—never. That is not how God intended it to be.

I began an escape plan to free myself, if only for a few hours. In reality, I should have been planning an escape for the girls and myself. I was hired at a local restaurant as a waitress, making new friends quickly. That gave me an excuse and valid reason to get out of the house. I soon found myself in Detroit a lot, with a coworker, Keisha. She lived in the city, and I occasionally gave her rides home. One particular Friday night, after getting paid, Keisha asked me to drop her at a local party store, so she could cash her check. My mind began to race and my wheels began to spin. I decided to cash my check too. In doing so, I was not going to have to ask permission for money. I took what I wanted, giving the rest to the household. I hated earning money and then have to grovel for some.

While in the store, I bought beer and Keisha would later buy weed from Floyd. It became our ritual after working on Friday evenings. The store clerk, Yousif, told me not to be a stranger, flirting innocently with me. Keisha was a regular, being the store was around the block from her home. Before long, I became a regular patron also. We began partying during the week, in addition to Fridays. I knew smoking weed interfered with my medications, but I did it to relieve my anxiety. Just like back in Knoxville. I had already been diagnosed for three years at that point. I felt I needed weed to calm myself down so I could prepare in going home. *Red flag!*

Being in the house with Pete was tough every day. I began smoking a lot of weed to get me through the slowly passing days. I had tremendous difficulty communicating with Pete regarding the basics. I was now facing major changes within myself and had no one to turn to. Keisha and I talked, but not on a higher level. I longed for Elizabeth and Whitney. I was all alone again. I felt totally abandoned by everyone.

I got a phone call, out of nowhere, one evening from Josie. We were shooting the breeze, and she out of nowhere said, "I want to let you know, Steve died." I broke down into a full stream of tears, asking "When are the arrangements?" "Oh! He died four months ago," she said unemotionally. "What?" I said crying. "Well, Mom didn't want you making a scene," Josie blurted out. I was silent and hung up the phone. I did not have another conversation with her for many years following that call.

Pete and I were beside ourselves in sorrow. The following week, I went to the cemetery office and paid for a vase on Steve's niche. He had been cremated. The cemetery had to phone my mom to get permission for the vase. There was no way I was going to make that call. *How cheap!* I thought. *Couldn't even pay for a vase for her husband. She would, most certainly, have no problem spending his money.* I cried frequently as I was extremely angry and felt shattered inside. I thought it unusually cruel of my mom to not let me say goodbye. She knew what Steve meant to me. At that point, I could not forgive her, and we did not talk for a long while.

I became somewhat self-destructive after Steve's passing. I was upset and did not seem to care about much anymore. I made a set schedule with Keisha. We both began going home every night together when we worked the same shift. Soon I began to stop drinking beer, and I only got high. Those were my coping skills for relaxation. My behavior became different;

however, I was no longer sweet Barb—I was angry all the time. I began having a short temper with everyone, including my daughters. I knew the home invasion and Steve's death made me feel hopeless. I was upset to not have any recourse whatsoever against Danny, Leslie, or my mom. Due to that fact, I became rebellious and extremely short-tempered in all of my actions.

At thirty-eight years old, I was displaying behaviors of a tied-down teenager. I was despondent to authority, responsibility, and life in general. I began leaving my home every evening, whether I worked or not. It was my breakaway from reality. I phoned a new therapist because Celia was simply too far away for me to drive. Crystal began to school me on my illness. She was also the one to diagnose me with Post Traumatic Stress Disorder. That label freed me immensely, making me realize the way I felt was due to the home invasion by my sister and mom. It was not my doing or my fault. That was liberating.

I wanted so badly to be myself again. However, I soon realized I never had a clear picture of who I was. I may have always been told by others, but I never knew. I had no idea what was happening. My bipolar was acting up, and I began to rapid cycle, mostly leaning toward the manic side. I was tired of taking on other people's garbage. At that time, something occurred within me. I began to be enlightened by God. I saw people for who they were, instead of how I perceived them to be. Pure enlightenment. I had a keen sense of heightened awareness.

At that same time, though, I felt desperate, and had reoccurring thoughts of death come over me. The thoughts engulfed me. Pete was being so unreasonable, and no matter what I did, it was not right. Pete began badgering me about every tiny thing I did wrong. I could not win. I was beside myself in personal anguish and was no longer thinking clearly; I began contemplating killing myself. I had a reel play in my head of all the things Danny and the rest of my born-into family had done to me. All the nasty, vindictive acts they perpetrated against me, I hated that. I hated them, and I lost track of loving myself. I was spiraling very rapidly and was fully coherent in knowing so. I had begun carrying a .25-caliber gun in my purse. I have no idea how I would have killed myself with that, but that was a plan of mine.

I always took rides in my car when I was upset. It was dark outside by the time I found myself on East Grand Boulevard heading toward downtown Detroit one night. *But why?* I thought. I found myself on top of the Belle Isle Bridge. I do not favor bridges or water. I was lucid enough to make a phone call to Yousif, telling him goodbye. I have absolutely no recollection after that. I only know what has been relayed to me from Yousif. My friend talked me off of the bridge for the moment. I then traveled six miles down to Hart Plaza, which sits on the banks of downtown and the Detroit River. I was determined, but Yousif called the police, warning them of my upcoming plans. The police were at Belle Isle and Hart Plaza, sitting in their patrol cars What are the chances of that happening in the city of Detroit? Slim! Once I pulled up in front of the fountain, which sat directly in front of where I was planning to jump, the police were there. I believe it was God's intervening and Yousif being a superb friend.

Somehow, I made it back home and slept. Yousif told me everything the next evening when I woke up. It seemed like a nightmare had taken place. I had been apparently ranting and crying about Pete and his abuse toward me. I was saying I should be gone to end the pain and anguish. Yousif told me what he thought I was worth. I listened that time. He proved the night before he was, in fact, there for me. I owed him my attention. Yousif was frank with me in telling me how he felt about who I was, and what I was on earth to do. He encouraged me and made me feel worthy.

Pete discarded me like you would a bag of garbage the following morning. Why? Just because I went to the Bahamas years prior? That made no sense to me. But that, as it was told to me, was the reason. I could not believe, of all times, the conversation was taking place now. I felt it was the worst possible timing. Pete was beating me down once again for something I had no remorse over. In my memories, I clung to that trip as the only good thing to happen to me in a very long time. I was determined that he would not strip me of that too. My dignity and self-esteem were all I gave. The memories? Those belonged to me.

> How long will I have anxious concern with grief in my heart,
> each day? How long will my enemy triumph over me?
> —Psalms 13:2

CHAPTER 25

I realized, in coming back home after being atop the bridge, I had many things to deal with. I was, a "fruit-loop and a wench" in addition to several other vulgarities. Wow! That was a lot to live down. Pete and I argued *every* day. He treated me as if I were there to serve him and pamper him. I was not in any shape to start taking care of a third child, and not at his age. I refused to be openly talked down to any longer, especially in front of my children. I had an epiphany after being atop that bridge. I knew I had to save myself instead of giving up. That meant I was going to have to get tough in my thinking. I scrambled to find out where to begin.

The way I was feeling now was lonely and desperate. My mom had begun coming back around occasionally to visit Melonie and Adaline, not me. That in itself was very stressful for me. She would make comments about my marriage, and even had the audacity to bring me *Marriage for Dummies*. At the time, I recall, feeling very sick toward my mom. At first, I felt it was a tradeoff, her seeing my daughters. I soon realized, though, she was an evil person whom I did not trust. I most certainly did not want my mom's personality rubbing off on either Melonie or Adaline. Secondly, I felt my daughters needed her, but in reality, none of us did. My mom was toxic. Before long, I told her not to come around any longer. I had to protect my girls. My mom, I observed, was a fake, narcissistic, just like Pete. *Red flag!*

I began looking for another job in 2007 and found a great position in the city of Detroit as an office manager/bookkeeper. The position was working at an electronics recycling company. I loved the job and many of my coworkers. The owners, two Jewish gentlemen, were wonderful to work for. They were fair, hardworking cousins. The job was not difficult for me mentally, and the people made it more enjoyable than that of a typical office. I was the only female working there, and thankfully, I always got along better with men. Women, as a rule, gossiped and cackled with and about each other. I was not that way. Within three months of beginning the job, I got a raise, making amazing money. I was able to pay my credit cards down. It seemed like a win-win situation. I soon ruined that. God was now tapping me on the shoulder once again. I was too wrapped up in myself to hear him.

    I began doing cocaine on my own, instead of occasionally with Pete. The amount of money that was being made, afforded the expensive luxury. I loved the feeling I got from it. When I was down, it seemingly, brought me up. Then I began to notice it was causing me to crash, only to wake again and continue the circle. I began stopping at Yousif's party store on my way home every day. If I did not stop there after work, it was at night, once dinner was finished. We frequently played backgammon together; he was an outstanding player. Yousif and I would chat about Pete and how I could learn to deal with him. He gave suggestions, and they were good. That was the capacity of our friendship. Yousif gave wonderful and usable advice, but he never told me to pack up and leave. I wish he had. I needed to hear that from an outsider.

    Then came my hint again to start saving my money, but I did not. My home life was not pleasant, other than the time spent with Melonie and Adaline. That time was becoming sparse though. I began to notice subtle changes in their personalities. Things that someone had to tell them, not things they naturally developed on their own. Those differences started coming to light. I was floored and taken aback. Melonie started to ignore anything I asked her to do. She became defiant toward me, telling me she did not have to listen to anything I said. I knew Pete was doing the unthinkable. He was persuading my daughters not to want to spend time with me. Pete had them believing I was a horrible mother and wife. Brainwashing was taking place; I saw it firsthand.

    Before long, Pete followed me to the store, ultimately confronting Yousif. Pete told him to "go *mess* with someone else's wife." Pete could not have been further from the truth. I was not interested in sex because of Pete, and Yousif was married. We were platonic friends, hanging out. Pete, in his twisted mind, figured I had to be having sex because I refused to let him touch me. I honestly was not interested in being intimate at that point in time. I knew what real love should feel like, and Pete proved he was not it. Yousif did a pretty good job insulting Pete too, and I felt Pete deserved every bit with all of his assumptions. I realized that must have been the way it began with Pete and his ex-girlfriend, Anna.

My daughters wanted less and less to do with me after that encounter took place. Melonie came to me and asked, "Why are you having an affair on Dad?" That was another pivotal moment that God brought to me, and I did not act on it. I should have been saving my money and making plans to leave Pete. I wish in hindsight I had *gotten* it. I was still thinking of marriage as a forever commitment. The insults continued on all levels within what was supposed to be my safe place, home. I was, once again, an outcast with my family. The bottom line was Pete was unable to control me, and he got vindictive. I wanted to break free but did not have a clue on how to get there.

Work became strained. I was putting in less hours due to not being able to concentrate. I was forgetting key functions of my job and could not understand why. Then, I realized, my medications were off again. Every time I went through something traumatic, they stopped being effective. Only that time around, I believed I made that happen with the amount of cocaine I had in my system. I knew better, but the everyday stresses were ganging up on me. I thought it was helping me cope; it was not.

I quickly checked into the psychiatric ward at the hospital, getting better within a week. I was unable to perform my job as described to me when hired. I knew I was going to leave within a short amount of time. I started going to lunch with all the salesmen on a regular basis. One day, I got inebriated and was not in any shape to drive home. I could barely stand, let alone hold my head up. I got a ride from a coworker to "sober up." We ended up at his house, where we had sex. I was so disgusted with myself as I drove home that afternoon. I could not fathom how I allowed it to happen. The following day at work was an embarrassment to both he and myself. We equally regretted what had occurred.

I always kept in touch with Boz, and now was a time I needed advice. He and I were now communicating through email, and I was lucky enough to have a few conversations with him via cell phone. Boz was brutally honest and gave me food for thought from a man's point of view. That helped me immensely, and I had no doubt he became my mentor. Boz never sugarcoated the facts, and I was about to get a lesson about the male species. At my age, I should have been taught or at least shown what was really going on in their minds. I learned of insecurities, shortcomings, and weaknesses. I never stopped to think how a man's mind thought differently than mine. I learned about narcissism and the need to control what is slipping away. Boz was describing Pete to a tee in that of his behaviors and mood changes. I was taught a great deal on that day.

Pete had been accusing me of having an affair for years. The fact was, because his last girlfriend cheated on him, he assumed I must be too. Pete's insecurities were getting the best of him. He began grilling me when I came home, overtly smelling me for men's cologne and throwing out tons of accusations. I had never been with anyone other than Pete during our fifteen years of marriage, until my coworker. But even before that incident, Pete went through my purse, my car, and even my personal items. I was so beside myself in misery; I had nowhere to turn other than therapy.

Pete took all of his suspicions to a whole new level. He escalated his invasion of my privacy. Pete continually went through all of my things: bags, boxes, purses, and pockets. Anytime he thought that I was hiding something, he searched those places. We were no longer sleeping together sexually; Pete inferred that I had to be "sleeping around because I was nothing but a hussy." He screamed to me that I was "not worthy of him or the person he was." That was truly funny to me, being I was treated the way I was. Pete began harassing me constantly; there was no mental relief. I was afraid to go home after work because it was always questionable as to what would be happening there. Sometimes, Pete was home from work before me; other times he picked the girls up without informing me. The head games were intense, enormous, and constant.

I was longing to do something for me, so I took up reading. I was often up later than I should have been. I stopped watching television and exclusively listened to the radio. I needed to feel good again. The TV was not cutting it for me. My time was open to spend with Melonie and Adaline. It began to be a routine that every time I wanted to spend quality time with the girls, they opted out, completely refusing. Why would they not want to be with me? They had turned into heavy TV watchers like their dad, and that was unfortunate for me. I wanted to bond over art, but they no longer wanted to hang out with me. There had to be a reason why, and I thought I needed to be proactive about it. It took some investigating on my end. I soon found Pete was trashing my character openly to the girls once again. At that time around, though, he was discussing *adult issues* with them. I knew it was very inappropriate and wondered what long-term effects it would have on them. The things I heard with my own two ears led me on journey to get the hell out. I had to save my psyche from being totally thrown off balance.

Pete thought he was slick; however, I thought him to be a backstabber who was habitually predictable in his anger patterns. I no longer could take his insults as they were so bad. I knew, by having my current position at work, I was capable of greatness. He was not about to strip me of that. Pete confronted me about having yet another affair on him. Yes, I slept with Joe from work, but I hardly set out for that to happen. To that point, I had not confirmed the affair with Pete. Evidently, Pete sent my underwear to the county lab and had them tested for male semen. They came back in a plastic bag marked positive. I was berated from there on out, eventually telling him what happened. He went to extremes to prove himself right.

Pete never treated me the same. He was a vindictive, coldhearted man who sought out to destroy me. He would kill me if he thought he could get away with it. He told me so. I was living in a hell of my own creation. I never tried to intentionally hurt Pete. The indiscretion with my coworker was just that, an extremely horrible lapse in rationality. I was not listened to on any level by any person in my home. I was being treated like an outsider yet again. God and I had conversations. I prayed to be able to get out. I should have been proactive, but never got the message in time. I was too busy being wrapped up in my own feelings; I unintentionally missed His words to me.

I did before long resign from my job. Beside the fact that I medically had to leave, the payroll was often not met. In addition, morale was substantially down and business was plummeting. Outside companies were not paying their bills. We were sinking. I left the job only to be unable to find work. My mind was being tested again due to the stresses of my home life. I was growing depressed due to Pete, not because of my mental illness. Pete loved getting under my skin, and unknowingly, I allowed it. In hindsight, I wish I had not partied to the extent I did. I should have put all the money away for a new life. God tried to instruct me, but I failed to listen. I was blind to see His guidance and deaf to His words.

> Go in through the narrow gate, because broad is the gate and spacious is the road leading off into destruction, and many are going through it; whereas narrow is the gate and cramped the road leading off into life, and few are finding it.
>
> —Matthew 7:13–14

CHAPTER 26

I struggled for two more years with Pete. I had a clear idea of what he was doing. I felt Pete was purposefully creating situations around to me with the hopes of having me "lose it" mentally. Little did he know, I was getting stronger and stronger every day. Emotionally, and more importantly, mentally. My depression was subsiding because I was growing more confident in myself, and in my thinking. I continued to party, smoking weed with different friends, including Keisha. It made me feel relaxed and able to face my life and fears. There were a lot of fears, and when I was high, I spoke up more freely without a filter.

Much time had passed between Pete and I fighting on a regular basis. We were not intimate in anyway; however, we spoke cordially to one another. I had been, for several years at this point, sleeping in the basement. It was not private by any means, but I had all my belongings with me. Melonie and Adaline were beginning to spend more time with me. We would go to the Detroit Institute of Arts. They both loved the arts, and it was something we all had in common. I clung to that.

Pete and I, on extremely occasional moments, partied with cocaine. He asked me to get it, and I did. It was an opportunity for Pete to be nice to the entire household. One Friday night, I bought a ball in Detroit at Pete's request, and took it home. Pete separated it before I went out for the evening. He made a snowpack for me, putting a portion in it. The whole time, looking back, Pete was odd. He was pleasant and nice, which of late he had not been either. I felt it suspicious inside; however, I dismissed it, giving Pete the benefit of the doubt. *Red flag!*

I took the snowpack with me to a hotel party that night. There were many people from Detroit whom I had not seen since working as a waitress. All of us partied for a while, and I engaged in a small amount of cocaine. There was too much reminiscing going on for me to really get into the partying. Many people began to leave; it was a perfect time to get reacquainted with a couple of friends whom I had not heard from in years.

We did the majority of the cocaine, leaving the packet almost empty. We had such an amazing visit; four of us ended up staying an extra hour after the first group left. I felt liberated again, happy to have decent people around me, accepting me. It was time to go, so I left, taking a wine cooler with me. I was not a drinker at all, but one of my friends handed it to me. It had been more as a joke because I was going back home. My buddy's thoughts may have been that I would eventually need it, having to deal with Pete.

About a quarter mile past the hotel, I got pulled over for no taillights. Apparently, they were not properly connected. I went to jail for possession of a dusting of cocaine, a small amount of weed, and an open liquor container. After probation, three days in jail, the lawyer fees, and over two thousand dollars' worth of fines, I was totally depleted, mentally, physically, and emotionally.

It does not take an engineer to figure out taillight bulbs do not just come loose. They are locked into place. Someone wanted that to happen, and it was with an evil mind-set that they became loose to begin with. I never accused anyone of doing it, but I knew who it was; the only person it could have possibly been. It was the same person who would assess, diagnose, and fix the problem: Pete. *What a dirty rotten individual*, I thought, *he must really hate me*. I did a great job from here on out to keep myself clean and out of trouble.

It was difficult to find a job now, even though the court case was resolved. I was thankful to God and the judge for the break in getting a 47-11 as the final ruling. That meant because I did not have a prior record, all the charges were expunged for me. Only the state police would be aware of the charges if I were to get pulled over in the future. I was relieved and happy. I hired a competent attorney. He was well-versed and did a fine job at getting the Open Liquor Container dismissed.

I never spoke of it to the girls. Pete said he had told them I was in the hospital for those three days. I never believed his story. I knew intuitively he told both girls exactly what I did. Pete ultimately orchestrated that night. I surmised the taillights were disconnected before, or possibly after, getting the cocaine. I also believe Pete had me purchase the drugs premeditating my demise. Nothing about that night was coincidental, except for seeing my friends.

Within days of the arrest, a supposed friend of mine spewed her hatred to the scout leaders. Lori was an extreme attention-seeker, but I had no idea she would turn on me. She knew of my court date and charges, not because I told her, but because her husband worked as a paralegal in the same office as my lawyer. I thought every word spoken to my lawyer was a private conversation. Little did I know, Stephen, Lori's husband, told her everything. That truly hurt me on many levels. Lori had an abortion a year prior, and I never said a word to anyone about her affair with her neighbor. It cut like a knife for her to betray me. She was supposedly my friend.

I was now banned from all scout meetings, and I no longer would be privy to trips with the girls. That was one of the hardest things I had taken away from me. I enjoyed all of the outings and the adult conversations. I felt miserable all over again. Even though I did all of it to myself with my partying, I never deserved the backlash I received. All those moms claiming to be my friends, and not one of them came to my aide. My mental anguish was heavy. I was being weighed down. I never hurt anyone; it was not my style. What was happening to me?

It proved to be a time to reach out to Boz for some much-needed support and advice. He was, as usual, there with wisdom only he provided. Boz was a real friend, and after five years of friendship, I wanted to go to Chicago to meet him. He declined the invitation, leaving me feeling heartbroken for the moment. I again came to realize men thought completely differently from women. Our minds were not on the same path. On the flip side, though, they ran parallel to each other, and I came to embrace our friendship as being from afar. Boz helped me to see, even as adults, we fall victim to others' pretend empathy. He made me realize I was not alone. What Lori did to me was comparable to being raped in my mind.

Approximately two years later, in the Fall of 2009, I had what I thought was a stroke. It started out as an anxiety attack, which escalated into my not being able to speak clearly. Soon my speech became severely slurred, and my left side went completely numb. I honestly thought I was paralyzed due to my not being able to move the left side of my body. An ambulance was called, and off I went to the hospital. Pete acted irritated and upset to have had to go through the hospital and ambulance scene once again. The doctor at the hospital had taken care of Melonie as a baby for a short while. He was, in my opinion, a quack, which is why he no longer took care of her. He told Pete, "It's all in her head." Well, it had been the second time I was hearing that remark and decided to give the doctor a piece of my mind. The goal was to embarrass him in front of his peers, and all I did was make myself look like the crazy one. The symptoms of having a stroke actually came from a reaction I had to one of the medications I was taking.

In the winter of the following year, I had what I describe as a nervous breakdown. I still do not have a clear picture as to say what really took place. I had my feelings, though, and they spoke volumes. At one point, and not feeling the least bit paranoid, I felt my medications had been tampered with. It was if I had cocaine in my system by the way I was feeling. I did an assessment on my medications, and there was in fact cocaine in my capsules. I never said a word to Pete, because it was clear he did it. I threw the capsules out, and from that point on, the refills went with me wherever I went. Finding the proper prescriptions to combat my illness were a Godsend. I did not need them to be *played* with in any way.

I was extremely aware and very lucid at this time because I was drug-free. I went so far as to call the police department in another city to ask questions about my meds. I found out, what Pete did with my medications was a felony. He could go to prison for that. After everything that man did to me, here was my payback. The only thing stopping me was I was the mentally ill one. I never wanted to step foot in our town's police department because they never treated me respectfully. I was spoken down to so badly over the years; there was no way I trusted them. They were afraid of my illness, I felt. I went to the local Michigan State Police office. They told me I could prosecute him. I had no proof other than to know they had been tampered with. It would be Pete's word against mine, and I was the one with the mental history.

Pete did, from there on out, harass, belittle, and verbally assault me even more than usual. It all centered around my illness and the affair. It became a way of life for Pete, a mission if you will. I believe he had a plan to get rid of me by all the misfortune I encountered. I feel it was a huge plot to gain sole custody of the girls. I was totally and completely clear-minded. I knew what was happening, but had no one to believe me and no one to turn to.

Pete continued his vicious behavior toward me, displaying it freely in front of and to our daughters. He openly referred to me as "it," and soon the girls followed. My suspicions about Pete putting me down to the girls had been confirmed. I do not care what kind of troubles a husband and wife have; children are to remain out of the equation. Pete was their "friend," and I was the disciplinarian. He referred to himself that way. Of course, they took their friends' side. It crushed me that Melonie and Adaline too had turned their backs on me. I had every possible person in my life betray me.

Therapy grew ever so intense. I kept looking for work, finally asking Yousif if he knew of anybody hiring. I was prepared to take any job. He sent me to an establishment owned by a friend of his. I went for an interview the following week and got the job. It was a step down in positions as far as pay and responsibilities; however, money was being made. I was productive again, and was doing labor that I mentally could handle. The medication reaction and breakdown had an effect on my brain. I felt differently.

I was now in charge of food preparation in a restaurant. It was all my mind was able to do at that point. I enjoyed the repetition of chopping vegetables, filling food containers, and cleaning all the food areas. Before long, I made and delivered menu items and decent tips poured in, simply because I was a girl. At that point, I should have told Pete I did not have a job, but that was not my style. Instead, I gave the majority of my check to the household, the rest going toward my credit cards. What a stupid move on my part. I should have been socking the money away. Pete became a real enemy in the house. When was I going to get the hints that God was overtly throwing in my face?

While hanging out in the city visiting Yousif, there was a man whom I began to chat with. Tiki and I spent many mornings together, getting to know one another. He was a local resident who kept the parking lots of party stores and restaurants cleaned from debris. I felt an old bond to Tiki even though we did not know each other. Call it kismet, call it God at work. Tiki had a friend, Papa Coot. Often, the two of them scraped near 6 Mile and Conant in Detroit. It was a popular job in the city, and they were really good at it. Papa Coot had a couple of dogs. They were vicious guard dogs who protected him. Even though Tiki, Papa Coot, and I considered ourselves friends, we only hung out on occasion. I also frequented Papa Coot's house with Tiki in tote when I did visit. We sat on the porch, petting his cat Justine and talking about our lives and challenges.

During my free time, I was taking care of the cemetery plots. It included all of my relatives and my grade school buddy, Paul. It became an opportunity for me to be away from Pete and still play in the dirt. Many times, Melonie and Adaline went with me. I showed them how gardening could be fun and rewarding. That particular year, I planned out our designs on paper. Melonie helped and Adaline assisted. It was so lovely a time. All that was about to come to a sudden and abrupt halt.

My eyes are always toward God, for he will free my feet from the net. Turn your face to my favor for I am alone and helpless. The distresses of my heart have multiplied. Free me from my anguish. See my affliction and my trouble; and pardon all my sins. See how numerous my enemies are and how violent their hatred for me. Guard my life and save me.
Do not let me be put to shame for I have taken refuge in you.
—Psalms 25:15–20

CHAPTER 27

On the Monday following Easter 2010, I finally got what I had been praying for but could never afford. I was served by the Macomb County Deputy Sheriff's office, an envelope with divorce papers. I looked at the deputy and wept because my happiness was beyond measure. Pete was doing so much drinking, which was nothing new, but he was becoming gutsy. Comments of nastiness and revolting insults flew from his mouth. His tongue was a dagger, his speech slurred. He came to the basement and assaulted me with spit and words, mostly screaming, *"Get out of my house. You're nothing but a hussy, and everyone knows it. You deserve to die!"*

In our state, it is the law, anyone filing for a divorce has to stay together for six months. It is a diversion to try to keep you in the marriage. Six months when you are being abused is six months too long. I wanted the divorce immediately. First, I had to find a lawyer, and I did not have any money. However, I was an expert of sorts at finding resources. I went to work to obtain a great lawyer who believed me and took my word in what I was being tormented with.

I prayed to be delivered by God. I prayed and sang to get me through. Queen recorded a great song, "I Want to Break Free." That tune, and Reo Speedwagon's "Time for Me to Fly" were my anthems. Even though I had things to keep my mind calm, the constant badgering was continued by Pete. I found myself, after researching some stores, a very cool and helpful spy shop. I purchased three sound-activated recorders. I figured, when a lawyer took my case, I needed to have tangible proof of the abuse.

During that time, the police considered me a threat. I had a long history with them, and none of it was favorable or accurate. There were, over the course of eight years, many calls *from me*, explaining the verbal abuse. Once to our house, they would comment, "Then get a divorce" or "He didn't do anything wrong...verbal abuse isn't against the law." I ended up getting arrested for domestic abuse on three different occasions when *I* called the police. "You touched me, there are handprints on my chest." On a hairy chest, you are going to see red marks. Pete was 6'1", and I 5'5". He was, I'm convinced, talking with the police outside of them coming to the house. I surmised he was stopping by the police station to give them "updates." I say that because those cops knew a lot about my circumstances. I wondered how.

It is quite laughable now, but then I was punished again and again for doing nothing wrong. I no longer had to worry about the police. I was getting my divorce. When going through such a mind-altering state as that of divorce, many things are said to intentionally hurt the other person. Pete crossed the line many times. That meant war in my mind. I was going to pay him back. I prayed again and again. I wanted God to show me a way to make it through the months ahead.

I began hiding the recorders one at a time. Pete's garage had to have one; he was in there secretly all the time. I put one in the kitchen: the common area, and the last went in my area of the basement. That night, once I left, the tapes proved to be informative beyond belief. Pete was talking horrifically about me. His mouth went on and on to his lawyer about my personality and how I was an adulteress. He degraded me to the girls, saying, "Your hussy mother cheated on me; I'm gonna get her back." In the basement, I recorded Pete going through my bags, unzipping them. All the while, he knew nothing of the recorders. I secretly recorded him for five months.

I had a meeting with two amazing women at the court building. They were from the abuse department, for divorce court. *What? There's a victim's unit for what Pete's been doing to me?* I shook my head, thinking it was all too unbelievable. These women walked me through the court process for the upcoming court date. The female judge was known for being highly intelligent, reading between the lines, and getting to the truth of the matter. I was excited because that is exactly what I needed.

I ultimately confided in those two gals, explaining the correlation between Pete and my born-into family. When they walked me into their private office, I burst into tears, tears of disbelief and awe. I walked briskly to her! Mrs. Beasley was sitting atop their desk, seemingly waiting for me. Here she was, after all those years. Her dress neatly pressed and her apron tightly made into a bow. I embraced her and cried. I explained what the doll meant to me. They were visibly moved.

I had a court date without an attorney. Once Judge Marta saw the tape in my hand, she said, "What do you have here?" That judge, with her tough disposition, let me play a portion of my cued tape in open court. The part I chose was Pete, telling Melonie and Adaline that "*It* deserves to die." The judge asked who "*it*" was, and I explained how Pete taught my daughters to refer to me that way. She lectured Pete for a good five minutes, noticing he was more in shock than remorseful. Pete's lawyer was taken aback and visibly upset. The judge immediately issued a restraining order against Pete, then told me, "Get a good lawyer." Pete got his lawyer from a large, full-sized ad on the back of the phone book. He was a ten-thousand-dollar lawyer, so I wondered where Pete's money was coming from.

After court, Pete was allowed to come back to the house with a police escort, for clothes. All hell was about to go down. Little did Pete know, not only was I clean from drugs and alcohol; I had my head on straight, and proved it in court. I was no longer going to let the abuse go on. It was almost like Danny all over again, taking advantage of me, to the point of unbearable discomfort. No more! I made some extremely important phone calls during the following week. I put my ducks in a row, and followed through with every one of my resources.

I found an attorney willing to take my case at no charge. That is correct. He was part of our county organization of resources, and they represented ten divorces every year. They chose mine to be one of those. There was a zero fee for Mr. George Bisser along with his expertise. He was young and handsome, with style and a demeanor to match. George meant business, all business; and he was not about to mess around with Pete or his lawyer. As my attorney, he never once asked to listen to the tapes. I felt mixed emotions about that in the beginning; however, I finally realized,

George had trusted in my word. That was good enough for me. The divorce was about to get very messy.

As if the household situation was not bad enough, I got devastating news from Yousif. Tiki had been hit and killed by a car. I was shocked, and honestly, I did not believe it. I had been through so much in my life, I could actually feel when something was happening. Here, I felt nothing, no pain. I went to Tiki's home and found he was in fact hit and dragged by a car on 7 Mile and Conant. He was alive but literally fighting for his life. We had been friends for a couple of years; I had to go to him.

I drove to Midtown Detroit to Receiving Hospital. I had to assess the situation for myself. Tiki had tubes running in and out of his nose and mouth. Seeing someone you care for in that predicament puts all the little stuff into perspective. Tiki was in the hospital for months recovering. Every opportunity I had; I went to see him. I prayed over his body, asking for God's healing light, to cleanse and heal all of his physical injuries. God did just that. Tiki was released before long, but it took him a long time to get back to being himself. He was completely repaired with titanium. He needed some time to recover from it all. I did, at that very moment, come to know why our friendship formed.

During the months following his recovery time, Tiki and I found ourselves frequenting the cemetery. He often cried, having flashbacks of the hit-and-run. He was now diagnosed with having Post Traumatic Stress Disorder, PTSD. I had the same diagnosis, so I talked Tiki though those times of anguish. At the cemetery, we gardened at all of my family's graves, seventeen in all. I believed it was an opportunity for Tiki to get his hands dirty, while creating beauty. Occasionally, we went to lunch, and he and I just chatted about court. Tiki kept telling me just how strong a woman I was and that the situation was God's will. He comforted me, and I did the same for him.

I had a court date a month later with the same judge. When I walked in with my lawyer, she seemed to almost have a little smile on her face. I was cool, calm, and collected. God was with me, standing beside me that morning. The clerk called me up to the bench and I quickly turned around, spotting the two women from the court abuse department. I felt empowered having those ladies around me. Mr. Bisser captivated the courtroom with his facts and made Pete and his lawyer look foolish. I was overflowing with excitement when it ended. Mr. Bisser made a great impression on me.

Tiki, Papa Coot, and I talked about Pete and my situation. Both men agreed communication is what was most important. Over the years, I had heard that. I agreed and realized Pete and I never had any type of ability to communicate well with each other. The only conversations going on between us were yelling, accusing, and belittling. I did my fair share too. After getting repeatedly attacked verbally and mentally, an individual can only take so much. I had a big mouth when it came to people putting me down.

Things became strangely calm in the house. Pete and I had something happen between the two of us that told each other it was all enough. God had stepped in. Pete acted like he understood what I had been trying to relay to him. The girls should not be involved. By now, though, it was too late. During those impressionable years, little minds are sponges. Both Melonie and Adaline had already taken to heart all the anger they witnessed and all the negativity toward me. Pete's good behavior did not last that long though.

By now, I was not expecting anything from the settlement except my girls, half of the belongings, and my cat. I knew I could not afford the house payments; there was no sense in fighting for it. But where would I live? That was something I never contemplated. Why was I walking through life with blinders on? I could not understand how I never thought of that. I was unprepared, having thought of everything, but the most important aspect. At that point, I just wanted to be free. I did not have many options with no one to turn to.

I had George stipulate in the divorce papers for me to be able to stay in the basement until I moved. The game plan was twelve months. Pete was a teeter-totter when it came to his emotions. He was never happy, only angry or unsatisfied. Now I wonder, *What the hell where you thinking, Barb?* All I really thought of was being around my daughters. I became sad at the thought of knowing I could not take them when I left. I would inevitably be homeless and on the streets after all. I could not have my daughters living out of the back seat of my car. Facts were, they did not want to go with me. They made that clear. I was beating myself up at every turn.

Pete and I walked into the courthouse, hand in hand, the day of our divorce. It was mid-October, and the air was crisp. I remember the feeling in my soul: elation and freedom! Pete asked me on the way in if I "wanted to change my mind." For the first time ever, I said "no," and felt great about it. The divorce was final, and we left the courthouse. I never looked back. I knew marriage was for better or worse, but God also instructs *not* to stay. I was being mentally and verbally tortured.

The two girls from the abuse department approached me at the end of the proceedings. They handed Mrs. Beasley to me as a gift. Apparently, the very deputy who was in the courtroom where my hearing had just been gave it to the abuse department. The girls asked the deputy if they could give it to me, and he said absolutely. I did get to thank him personally and told him my story. Apparently, the deputy was also abused when he was younger. It was a victorious moment in my life. Everything was finally coming together. But where was I going to live? I wish I had Elizabeth or Whitney to turn to.

Now that everything was finalized, Pete was back to being nice. The final settlement was fifty-fifty custody. I did not want my girls to grow up without a dad in their lives like I did. We were all under the same roof again, despite the fact that Pete and I were divorced. My medications were working well, and I was feeling great. I did not want any altercations with Pete ever again. I knew, though, it was only a matter of time. After all, I had a clear picture of Pete. His personality was that of an angry victim who was a habitual liar. I had to stay alert.

One night, Pete asked me to party with him "for old time's sake." I said no. Quickly, he turned against me. I knew I had one year to get out; I needed a good job, but could not get a break. I was still at the restaurant, only a different location. I was not making enough money to support myself, let alone the girls. I applied for disability but did not hear anything. Depression was setting in again, and I could not afford to visit that mood.

One day the phone rang on the landline. I knew the voice immediately, although I had not heard it in nearly twelve years. It was Whitney, asking if it was "Barb's residence." I excitedly screamed out loudly, "Yes, Whitney, it's me." We both busted out into laughter and tears, and immediately got together for dinner within a week.

We caught up with one another, making sure not to lose touch again. Whitney had four boys, and she was also divorced. We had a wonderful visit.

Things had changed, though, and I was not the same person. I explained everything to Whitney, and she still accepted me. She did comment once I told her about my born-into family, "They always treated you badly when we were growing up." Wow! That was a pivotal moment in my recovery. I never had that validated before. No one had ever been in a position to tell me that.

Whitney and I spent a lot of time together; however, I was still hanging out with Yousif, on occasion playing backgammon and unwinding. The tension in the house could be cut with a knife. Pete always said, "The girls are too young to know what's going on. They're fine." Well, they were not and I could see it. Both Melonie and Adaline refused to go to therapy, and I knew Pete's opinions, were rubbing off on them. The facts were, they both needed to be able to talk with someone who was objective.

Not that I am saying this because I am in need, for I have learned to be self-sufficient regardless of my circumstances. I know how to be low on provisions and how to have abundance. In everything, and in all circumstances, I have learned the secret of both how to be full and how to hunger. Both how to have abundance and how to do without. For all things, I have the strength through the one who gives me power.
—Philippians 4:11–13

CHAPTER 28

Pete and I began arguing and fighting about old topics. While I slept one evening, he was upstairs getting inebriated yet again. I learned to ignore him by pretending to sleep, but it did not stop his mouth from running. I felt no need to spar any longer. Pete was up to his old bickering that particular night, and he turned physically violent on me. He was trying so hard to get me to go off on him. But by now, God had guided me to be still in my anger, and I had been. Pete came over to the couch, proceeding to dig the heel from his right foot into my shin with full pressure and force. I could feel the bruise welting up immediately. It was quite a massively large area that was affected, and tender to the slightest touch. I quickly got dressed and went to the police department. They refused to make a report saying, "I don't see anything on your leg."

Without a beat, I moved out the very next day, temporarily staying with a friend. Another dumb step, because Pete moved right in to that situation and took full advantage of me. It proved to be a bad move all the way around with Pete and Dina, my so-called friend. She, after moving me in, decided to pick a man over our current agreement, letting him move in too. That forced me out. Now I was out of Pete and Dina's houses, having nowhere to go. I wanted to take Melonie and Adaline with me. I could not have them sleeping in the car with me when they had their own beds.

I moved all my things from Pete's into storage. Everything I had owned, and all the items I won in the divorce were in a locked unit. At that point, I was homeless and did not have my girls. I hated not taking Melonie and Adaline, but I had no family or friends to help me. It did not take long until I was sleeping in my car every night. Melonie and Adaline were eleven and nine at that time.

I changed every day at my storage area, and I bathed inside a local restaurant's bathroom. Pete knew nothing about my living arrangements and thought I was couch-surfing. On occasion, I may have been privy to that luxury, but those days were few and far between. My friends did not have room, and they were raising their own children. It would have equally been upsetting to me to be there, not having my girls with me. I got used to living that way. I had a routine and stayed in my storage during the day, so as to not waste gas driving around. When I did go out, it was to see Papa Coot, Tiki, or Yousif. Many days, I was in the library reading the latest news on bipolar.

I was three months behind on my storage rent and did the unthinkable. I took and pawned eight hundred and eighty dollars' worth of jewelry from Yousif's home. I was house-sitting and carried out the unthinkable, removing a bag of jewelry from the kitchen. When confronted by Yousif, I coward down and denied taking it. I lied to my friend who had been there for me, when I, at my lowest, had his support. He was actually the only one who tried to help. The police were already involved; it was just a matter of time. As a few days went by, I wanted so desperately to confess to Yousif. My heart and soul wanted to tell him what I had done, but my ego and fear prevented that from happening. I eventually got found out but not caught until eight months later.

During that time, and being I was on the run, I had to tell Pete what was going on. I thought I was going to go to jail for a long time. Yousif's wife claimed more was missing than that of what I took. It was crystal clear to me she was lying for insurance purposes, but I was in no position to make any assumptions. Pete acted like he was there for me, but he was not. What did I expect? Talk about total ignorance and shame. I was so sickened with myself. I was on the run, staying in shelters on occasion or in my car. I was afraid of getting caught, and I thought my sentence would be too insurmountable to handle. I knew if that occurred, I could certainly become mentally unstable. It was bad enough being homeless and totally alone.

I was so miserable on the inside all the time. Even though I had nothing, I still had God. He and I had long conversations about everything. I repented. We talked about my goals and dreams, and I had never felt so close to Him before. I prayed and meditated on why I was in the predicament and what I could do to change my situation. I asked what I was supposed to learn from it all. God told me patience. I laughed because I had never had that quality. I was not in the habit of shutting God out, so I listened and did what He instructed.

I was eventually picked up in St. Clair County, which is outside of Port Huron. I was staying in an abuse shelter at the time while waiting to hear from disability and the police. On my way to the shelter, a K9 unit sheriff pulled me over. Evidently, it is illegal to travel a country road expressway in the left lane. I never knew that. The sheriff was nice; it was the first time a dog would not be kind to me. The shepherd smelled me. He was still in the back seat of the SUV patrol car, but I had nothing on me. He was barking and growling. A half hour earlier, while in my car, I swallowed two dime bags in the plastic as to not leave anything in the car. I had been waiting for the sheriff to call on the warrant.

I was transported to St. Clair County. There I waited for several hours until the local police arrived, taking me to my county jail. I was dazed, literally for three days, sleeping nearly all of the time while incarcerated. In the county jail at that time, you were not able to make collect calls to cell phones. They accepted landlines only. There were two numbers I knew by heart, and I called both of them, Pete and my mom. I had to take the walk of shame for bail money, asking my mom. Pete said he did not have the cash, but I knew he did. He wanted to punish me by keeping me in jail. My mom, two calls later, ultimately put up a thousand dollars, and I was free. I was immensely thankful to her expressing it through my tearful words. She was cold and super short with me, showing it through her fake smile and stern words.

Pete did call my mom at some point while I was locked up because they came together to bail me out. I was honest with my mom about what I had done. Why would I lie? Today, I believe Pete told her anyway, but it did not bother me. Pete took me back to my car, which at that point was at his house. I had called him when I got pulled over and he and Paddy got the car back safely. I visited with the girls for a short amount of time before leaving for the night. Then I looked for somewhere to sleep. My storage area was not an option because they did not allow that, and it was late in the evening by that time.

For the night, I slept in a local hotel parking lot, in my safe and quiet car. I was so thankful to be out of jail. Melonie and Adaline were happy to see me when I got to Pete's. I fell asleep to that thought in my mind. The following day, Yousif and I met. I explained everything to him, and he understood. He was extremely disappointed in me for the action; however, he knew what kind of person I really was. Yousif forgave me, and we continued to be friends. Pete had big issues with that. Yousif forgiving me was what I needed. He believed in me, and knew it was a lapse in judgement, not a character flaw.

I was assigned a court-appointed lawyer. She was not only useless in my eyes; she had no real interest in taking my case. I could tell when the judge assigned it, she was very aloof. Nonetheless, she represented me for two court dates. The charge was theft in a building: a felony. It was talked down to a misdemeanor, with eighteen months of probation, restitution, and community service. I was relieved and satisfied with the punishment. I got what I deserved.

In the summer of 2012, while driving to see Melonie and Adaline, I felt the need to pull over into a parking lot. There I sat with tunnel vision and a pounding headache. The tunnel was black, becoming smaller and smaller until I could not see. Once I became aware again, I was sitting in a parking lot, my car still running. I do not recall how much time elapsed. I called my psychiatrist immediately. I was instructed to drive to her office if I felt I could. Upon arriving, I was immediately informed I had a toxic reaction to one of my medications. I not only had to discontinue it; I needed to be hospitalized for one week. I was happy. I felt I had to have some type of change in my medications, but never imagined it would be due to toxicity. I was, after all, under much stress being homeless. I was not scared or embarrassed; I was worried and had much guilt in my heart and on my mind.

The hospitalization was an enlightening experience for me. My mind was aware and coherent. I was lucid and self-sufficient while I was there. Attending groups and being prescribed a new regiment of medications worked well for me. I felt good after four days, and my mind was able to process the new information they were telling me. Yousif and I spoke every day. At the end of my stay, on a Sunday morning, I looked at the clock on the narrow hallway wall, and it was quarter after ten. I had a huge smile on my face, anticipating Yousif's arrival to break me out.

Once Yousif came to get me, we first went to the doctor's office to get my car. I quickly made it over to see the girls. Melonie, Adaline, and I spent some quality time together, and my girls were happy I was not in the hospital anymore. They told me they could see I was happier, and I really was. It was because of the medications and group meetings giving me control over myself again. I left to find a spot for the night and told my daughters I was coming back on Tuesday. Yousif and I were getting closer and deeper as friends. I began to share my dreams with him. He was a good man, and he realized I was a good person.

> For man is born for trouble, as surely sparks fly upward. But I would appeal to God, and to God I would submit my case. To the one doing great and unsearchable things. Wonderful things without number. He gives rain to the earth and sends water upon the fields. He raises the lowly up high, and he raises up the dejected one to salvation. He frustrates the schemes of the crafty, so that the work of their hands does not succeed. He catches the wise in their own cunning so that the plans of the shrewd are not thwarted.
>
> —Job 5:7–13

CHAPTER 29

Tuesday afternoon, while at Pete's home, Leslie called. Yes, my sister whom I had not spoken to in ten years was on the phone. She asked me if I was sitting down, and I said, "Has mom died?" "No, it's worse," she managed to say as her voice quivered. "John has committed suicide; he shot himself in the head." I literally fell to the floor, screaming and weeping for Johnny. Melonie and Adaline rushed to me, holding me tightly. I called Pete immediately, and we both wept.

Leslie's daughter Mary, along with my mom, came to pick me up at Pete's within minutes. We were all going to North Carolina to bring John home for a proper funeral. That, of all things, was what they chose to include me in on. I was happy to be going. After all that time had gone by, I was ready, so I thought, to handle my born-into family. They created many demons in my life, and signified hate, fear, and self-loathing. They gave me guilt, shame, and unlovingly failed to nurture me. I was not prepared nor could I have fathomed what was to come. My new medications were sure to get a good workout in protecting my psyche now.

I was taken to Leslie's house, where I became surrounded by all people who were overwhelming to me. My niece and nephew were all grown, my brother-in-law was all gray, and they were all acting like they had authentically missed me. It was very strange indeed. I called Yousif, telling him I was on my way out of town with them. He made subs for us at his store, and I took them for the road trip. It was all I could contribute since I had no cash.

In Leslie's front room, I told my mom I had court the next day and could not go. My mom called the court for me and explained everything to the judge's clerk. Leslie, Mary, Danny, and Patrick walked into the room. They heard the tail end of my mom's conversation, pressing us for information. I told them briefly what happened. That was a huge mistake! They treated me like they cared, and I fell for it hook, line, and sinker. They played me yet again. Every single person, except Mary, had something to say though. It was not as if I did not already feel terribly about it. I was there for all of twenty minutes and was being bashed. I had just gotten out of the hospital with a new attitude, and they were squashing it very quickly. *Where is Henry?* I thought. He would rescue me.

We all got into Danny's SUV and drove to bring John back to Michigan. On the way, we stopped in Knoxville, picking up Josie and Brenda for a caravan. I personally felt Brenda had no business coming, but she did. It was supposed to be the five siblings and my mom. However, Josie informed us once we arrived Brenda was her "moral support." We were in no position to argue the point, and she knew that. Henry and I sat together in the back of Danny's truck. It was an additional three hours to the hotel in North Carolina. There were a lot of facts being discussed about John's suicide, but for me, it was all speculation. I knew my family and their ways. There were moments of silence when all I heard was my own sobbing. Henry held my hand, crying too.

All of us went to the funeral home, even before going up the mountain to check into the hotel. The town we were in was an extremely small and a very Southern community. Before long, everyone it seemed knew who we were and what we were doing there. John and Lynn were professionals in this tiny municipality. Lynn was a doctor now, and John was a master woodworker and craftsman. They lived on the top of a hill, in a three-quarters-of-a-million-dollar home. They were well known. Plus, as we learned, John had extreme issues with paranoia. He had an elaborate camera system encompassing his property, which was installed in recent months. I thanked God there were no cameras in his workshop where he killed himself. I was informed John was acting extremely paranoid in and around the community.

More details emerged once we got to the sheriff's department. We found that John died Sunday, following a walk down the path of his property to his workshop. The time? Quarter after ten in the morning! I cried and cried. I was anticipating my hospital release at that moment. John, he was making a sick mind's judgment call, one that he could not take back. I was not at all mad at John. I suffered too; however, he suffered silently, and he did not have to.

My mom always raised us with a stigma toward mental illness. John knew how I had been treated over the years by our family. He and I were in regular contact. I surmised John did not want medications because it signified weakness within our upbringing. Admitting a problem was a problem in itself. John was a wealthy, strong, and reformed man. So, everyone thought. The subject goes much deeper and more will be extrapolated in these pages.

Once we were all inside the funeral home, the family started ganging up on me because I was speaking up. They expected Henry and Danny to do all the questioning. The girls were brought up that way; I did not believe in that philosophy and refused to stay quiet. I had things to get off my chest, and I was going to get answers before leaving. There was not one valid reason for me not to talk, so I did. I wanted details of where John was. Since they were notified of our impending arrival, no action of his body could be taken. We were then told he was "on ice" in the cooler.

I insisted on seeing John's body, and everyone warned against it. My mom became appalled by me. *Tough!* I thought. None of those people knew me anymore. I quickly pulled Henry aside and I explained to him, "If I see John, I know I would never try to commit suicide again." When Henry heard me say *again*, he looked at me with his steel hazel eyes. I was not trying to convince everyone they had to see John; I wanted to view him for myself. Henry knew what I was doing; he understood even though he did not agree. Or did he?

Henry took my side; however, everyone else was against my going into the funeral home garage. We did view the body and all the disagreements were done, for the moment. Danny, Henry, and I walked up to John's remains and examined the gun shoot wound plus the surrounding area.

Josie, Leslie, and my mom got a glimpse and broke down. I got a lot of flak for that. Henry cried and wiped his tears away. Danny stroked his chin, turned to John's body, and said, "You're not a man." I told him to "back off," but he refused. He was degrading a dead man with a mental illness. You really do not get any lower than that, or any more ignorant!

Henry and I walked away, and Josie came over and put her arm around Danny. That was so strange to me. As we sat on the brick wall surrounding the funeral home, arguments ensued and strangers started to take notice. Danny began putting me down, and I started calling him a child molester. I told him, "Now back off!" He finally did, after some additional words with many vulgarities were exchanged, and Henry finally stepped in. I got into Josie's Jeep, and off we went to the hotel. The insults were flying everywhere, none of which were coming from my mouth.

Once back at the hotel, everyone dispersed and I went to lay down. I was okay, but overtly exhausted. I declined dinner with the family, staying in the room. That night, my mom slept with me on the sofa bed, and we comforted each other. We chatted for a while, then I fell asleep to my mom whispering, "I love you, Barbara." I had a warm and comforting feeling come over me. My mom, after everything I had done, loved me. I was happy.

The tone of the following morning was quiet after all the day before had brought. I did not get a chance to speak to anybody once I woke up. All the women shared a room, and we all had gotten dressed. My born into family came into my room and all of my siblings, with the exception of Henry, took turns bashing me. They were all lined up against the wall pointing their fingers, swearing vulgarities. They said things that were fighting words. Josie, of all people, called me a "hussy," Danny was insulting me about being on public assistance while waiting for disability. "What a lowlife you are. You should be disgusted with yourself" were his words. Well, I was not, but I knew he was a child molester, and nothing could change that fact. Leslie was talking about my daughters and how "I'm hurting them." That comment, coming from her, it did not hold much water with me. My mom did nothing to stop, or intervene in stopping, their behavior toward me. They attacked me for well over two hours. Even though my mom did not say anything, her silence, along with her face expressions, spoke volumes to me.

Danny told me to "take my welfare *butt* back home." Oh! Did I want to leave? Then my mom chimed in, "You've got to go." "You people bring me all this way to degrade and humiliate me. It did not work. You all are messed up in your heads" was what I shouted out. Every last one of them left the room and went to lunch, leaving me there alone. I called Whitney, crying uncontrollably. When they came back, I had a Greyhound ticket waiting for me, thanks to my dear friend. She told me to "Get the hell away from those psychotic people." I could not have agreed more.

When everyone returned from eating, they were quick to send me on my way. My mom, with a smirk in her voice, said, "You're taking the Greyhound home" and handed me the exact change, in cash, for a ticket. I already had my bag packed; Whitney and I already had a plan. Just like that, I left the room and was gone, not even saying goodbye to Henry. I went to Josie's Jeep to get my sweater, and Brenda and my mom followed behind me. Brenda had no words to say in the situation because she was just a young adult. She had no idea what the depth of my family's dysfunction was all about, and she had no clue how cunning and narcissistic they all were. Their behavior was normal for her, and she accepted it as so.

My mom and I exchanged words. I told her, "You're a sorry excuse for a mother. John died because of you, because you are in denial and didn't get him help." I also recall screaming, "You, you have never done anything for me…you are not my mom anymore." My mom said, "Oh, really? I've never done anything for you?" I, in a deeply sarcastic voice, told her "not until recently." With that being said, I got in a cab that they prepaid for, and the driver took me to the bus station. My body shook physically as we drove away. I knew I was done with my born-into family. I felt it was finally over. Over? Yes, in the sense that I did not want to deal with them, ever again. That was the last time I would ever see any of them. From here on forward, I spoke to Henry and his wife Lydia only.

The bus trip was long, and while onboard, the driver announced a layover in Knoxville for twelve hours. If it had not been for the cash from my mom, I could not have stayed in an economical hotel. I had the cab driver take me to Merchant Road, my old stomping ground for a night's rest. After a long hot shower, dinner, and a beer, I called Yousif and Whitney, explaining where I was. Whitney was relieved I was gone from my family and their unhealthy grip. I had a very restful sleep and woke the next morning bright and early.

On the bus trip home, Pete called me distraught, telling me how his buddy since high school, Marco had passed away. Marco was a great guy who succumbed to an illness from pill addiction. In addition to John's death, we had another to deal with. Pete took John's death extremely hard. Marco's compiled the difficulty tenfold for him. I did not have any clue how I was going to come back from the brink of insanity. I was crying in sadness, and I was not sure how to handle myself.

Yousif picked me up from the bus station that evening. He embraced me, comforting me. "Everything's going to be okay now," he whispered. I knew what he was trying to do; however, I was such a wreck; it was hard to see anything good ever happening again. I had enough money left over to afford a cheap hotel for a week. Yousif dropped me off, and I checked into a room. The next morning, I did two urgent things. I called my therapist and the court clerk. I made appointments with both. My therapist, Josh, and I met the next day.

Josh was a Godsend to me in many ways, and not just with helping me through John's death. He taught me and inspired me to do better. Josh gave me the mental tools to deal with my family's toxicity. I was totally alone now. No family, no husband, and no home. I was truly struggling to keep my head above water. Deep down inside, I knew I was a strong and resilient soul. I, in my own mind, refused to sink, and I became determined to prove them all wrong. I clung to my faith in God, and the fact that He had me here for a purpose. I recalled all the great tools I had learned while in the hospital, and I began to incorporate the ones I liked into my daily living. I did have my daughters through all of these ups and downs, and that meant everything to me. Perhaps not their undivided love, but they were mine. My heart really was filled with love, as it always was, but with a newfound twinkle. Melonie and Adaline, who meant the world to me, were now to be protected from my born-into family.

The court date came, and my lawyer, Ms. Thom, showed no interest in me or my case. She did a poor job in front of the judge. Ms. Thom gave him ample reason to throw the book at me, and he did. The judge looked at the claim that all the jewelry was in fact taken. Everything she said was missing, was put on me. I was in shock and dismayed. I literally had just been mentally beaten by my family and now I had to deal with the news from the court. I wondered how I would find the ability, within my mind, to fight back. I should have fought for what was right and just, but my body was exhausted, and I could not gather the energy to intervene and represent myself. The judge did not see the lawyer's incompetence, and that infuriated me. I could not speak.

The court ordered me to pay twenty-six thousand dollars, not the eight hundred and eighty dollars that I had actually pawned. I really lost it in court. My lawyer smiled, as if to say, *My job is done*. I refused to pay for her services. I then, weeks later, issued a complaint against Ms. Thom's representation of me to the court. I went to the clerk's window and explained my issue with her. I refused to pay for such substandard representation. When I turned around, there stood Ms. Thom. I smiled and walked away.

In addition to paying for drug drops, I had court costs and now an astronomical amount in restitution to pay. Yousif and I talked in detail about that afterward. He knew I did not take the other jewelry. I wondered why he was so certain. Although I was beside myself in anguish, I followed through with everything I could do. All that was within my power I did, and that began with community service. I decided to help a local food bank. I found it so rewarding, helping others in need, who were worse off than I was. God knew I was humbled and thankful for what I did have. Here I was helping the less fortunate who needed food and I was in need of housing. My car was comfortable though. I could not complain.

It was a cold, wintery afternoon, and I was selling papers for the food bank, as part of my community service. I did the crime; it was my responsibility now to do what was ordered of me. I was in a grocery store, meeting and chatting with people who stopped to buy papers. One lady in particular was in a hurry, so I just said, "Merry Christmas!" She turned, looking at me for a split second. With a question in my voice, I said, "Mrs. Nickie?" "Yes," she turned to me and smiled. "Mrs. Nickie from St. Louis the King?" Her smile grew bigger. "Who are you?" I told her my name, explaining to her how I prayed to see her again. She was grinning from ear-to-ear, stopping for a moment to chat. I talked quickly as I recalled she was hurried. I told her what she had done for me while I was growing up.

No longer rushed, she listened, ending the conversation with a hug, a kiss, and her phone number.

The reason I'm sharing that with you is because Mrs. Nickie and I would never have met had I not been on probation. I never frequented the establishment where I was. God is constantly working on our behalf, even in the worst of circumstances. We have to have faith, believe in prayer, and actually pray in a bold way. Months flew by, and I often thought of calling Mrs. Nickie but did not. I felt I had said everything to her. I had contemplated that moment happening after all. By prayer and truly believing in the power of God, I got to say exactly what I wanted to.

Just before Christmas in 2012, Pete's twin, Paddy, was rushed to the hospital. He was having a hard time breathing. Pete was crazy with worrying, and Mara escalated the panic. Apparently, there were blood clots involved and tough decisions had to be made. Paddy slipped into a coma. It was heart-wrenching to see him so strong one day and brain-dead the next. Pete was never so beside himself. He was hard to console, but I did my best to be there for him. Mara prolonged the inevitable by not letting Paddy go to sleep peacefully. I could never know how I would personally act if that happened to me; however, I have an action plan. Paddy and Mara should have had that also. The autopsy stated that the death was blood clots to the heart, but I believe he died from a broken heart. After Paddy passed away, Pete had a whole new set of mannerisms: Paddy's. Pete became a verbal fire talker.

I hooked up with an old girlfriend whom I had been friends with years earlier. Sara said I could stay with her at her trailer until my disability came in. I was so excited to have someone willing to help me. Truth was, even though I did not consider myself a thief, I was. I continued to get the best therapy, and I grew stronger and more confident every day. The only issue I had with myself was that there was no way of working any longer. My concentration skills were minimal, and I found it very hard to be in crowds. Anxiety was a huge part of my bipolar symptoms. I was on special meds, in addition to my psychotropic medications. It did, in fact, relieve my anxiety once I let it take effect.

Sometimes, calming down and breathing is the best thing for the situation. Your thoughts and innermost feelings that your body is experiencing are crucial. You must give thought, deep thought, to those points. Going to your *happy place* during that, or any mental health crisis, honestly relieves symptoms within seconds. Afford yourself the luxury of that doing it for your own health. It is free, and you get to go wherever you would like. I am forever grateful to Christine Landino for teaching me these tools.

After waiting a long, extended period of time, I ended up with an attorney for disability and finally received my monthly amount. I never felt guilty for applying and obtaining those benefits. I had been working and paying into the system since I was seventeen. I was authentically sick. I was not brought up to accept or ask for assistance. Yet, I needed many of the government programs available to a homeless, mentally ill person. Truth be told, if you have not been employed at a job making at least fifteen dollars an hour, for many years, you are going to receive the minimum allotment for disability benefits.

I was not able to live off of the amount given to me, and I could not work to gain more money. Yet another obstacle for me to face. I did find myself laughing at my circumstances many times. I knew there had to be something better for me out in the world. I continued praying for brighter days when the struggle would be over. I also had a bright outlook for my future. I figured God had me go through the terrible storm in my life for a reason. It would come to me when He was ready, and when I was open to hearing Him.

> Instruct me in your way O God, lead me in the path of uprightness
> because of my foes. Do not hand me over to my adversaries,
> for false witness has risen up against me, and they have treated
> me with violence. Where would I be if I did not have faith,
> that I would see God's goodness in the land of the living.
> —Psalms 27:11–14

CHAPTER 30

Henry and his wife, Lydia, were constantly in my life. Although we did not chat as often as I wanted, we did reach out to one another frequently. Lydia called one day, and we stayed on the phone for hours. She was mailing out a card to me and told me what a great person and sister I was. I was touched beyond measure. I felt that same way about Lydia. Within a week, the card arrived. It had quite a large check in it. It contained part of my inheritance from John's estate; I honestly was not expecting anything. Divine intervention!

Danny, Leslie, and Josie put up quite a fight with Henry about how I was to spend my share. Henry told them, "It's none of your business how she spends her money, it's her money." I loved him for coming to my rescue. I had not spoken to anyone in my family, except for Henry and Lydia, since John's passing. The truth was, those people knew nothing about me or my life. They had no right to know and I was sure to keep it that way. However, that certainly did not detour them from gossiping about me.

I paid off all of my court costs, probation costs, and eight hundred and eighty dollars in restitution to the court. The additional twenty-six thousands dollars was not going to be paid by me. I refused. I was near completion of my probation when it was cut short. I knew it was because the court got their money; that was all they cared about. I was so relieved to have that ongoing weight finally lifted off my shoulders. I was completely free from probation and had no reason to go back to the court. I wanted to keep it that way indefinitely. I would vow to keep my nose clean from here on out. I also made a pack with myself to never take the walk again. I never wanted to be incarcerated, for any reason!

It had been an extremely cold season, so I kept an eye on Tiki and Papa Coot. I frequented the east side of Detroit to visit them. Even though they both had homes, they often scrapped and did not pay attention to the weather. One afternoon, I went to see Papa Coot at his home and bring him his favorite cold-weather drink, vodka. His dogs, Cena and Sampson, were vicious animals. They had a specific job. They guarded and protected Papa Coot. I heard them inside, but Papa Coot never came to the door. I went home for the evening.

That night, we had a snowstorm, and over twelve inches came down. It steadily fell until the early morning. The following day, I picked Tiki up, and he and I went back to Papa Coot's. Tiki had not seen him either, nearing three days. There was still no answer at the door. We shoveled the snow vowing to come back later in the day. Upon returning, I went to the door. Tiki shoveled the last inches that had accumulated while I knocked. Papa Coot called out, "Barb, help! Help me, Barb!" I yelled to Tiki and continued talking to Papa Coot through the door. He answered me and then…silence. The door was locked, so Tiki broke the window, getting inside quickly. There was Papa Coot curled up in the corner of the living room, with only a T-shirt on and a blanket wrapped around him. His house was freezing inside. Cena and Sampson laid on top of him, keeping him warm. Tiki knew the dogs very well, and there was no issue with him going inside. Tiki carried Papa Coot to my warmed van as we all got inside. I asked Papa Coot several times if he wanted to go to the hospital. I evidently had not gotten a very good look at him. Upon really checking his hands out, God tapped me on the shoulder, telling me to go immediately and quickly to the hospital.

Papa Coot was admitted to Receiving Hospital in downtown. When I called the next day, the nurse had informed me, being I had brought him in, that "his life was first and most importantly saved." I began crying because I knew it was bad news. Papa Coot was going to have one leg amputated that day. I was so heartbroken. Apparently, he had suffered severe frostbite. Three days following the time he was taken to the hospital; Papa Coot was ready for visitors. Tiki and I went to see him. In hindsight, I should have gone alone, but Tiki and I were equally worried.

It was much worse than predicted. Papa Coot had to have both legs removed well into the upper thigh area. Every single digit from his hands were also taken. We all cried together that day, and Tiki took it especially hard. Papa Coot is an amazing soul though. I knew he would overcome that season of tribulation. Then he began to cry, "I guess I'll never play basketball again!" I chuckled. "Not only will you play basketball, you'll have a great pair of brand-new legs." Papa Coot was my friend. There was no way in the world he would ever be forgotten. I was making it my personal duty to be sure he was properly cared for from here on out.

Therapy was going quite well for me and with a new therapist. Josh had been promoted from within the organization. I followed up with a couple of female therapists over the next few months. Their individual teaching styles proved to challenge me. They stretched my mind, taking me to new places. I learned many new techniques on living life again. I came to realize Pete was who he was, just like my siblings. I did not need any of them in my life, and more importantly, I did not need their validation. I learned to surround myself with people who authentically cared for me and about me. I felt I was worth more than the love I received, and I learned it did not have to come from my family. It was liberating, knowing I had total control over my own existence. There is no feeling like that. I now needed housing and concentrated exclusively on that.

I was actively looking for an apartment or home to rent, but was unlucky because of my criminal past. I learned the first thing the landlords pulled up on me was theft in a building/felony. What? That was not true though. It had been reduced down to a misdemeanor, had it not? I went to the library and immediately got on the computer. Sure enough, it said felony. I went back to the probation officer and she had it corrected. Even though it was now a misdemeanor, I still could not find a place to live. Every place I felt was a fit for my needs refused to accept me. I was down, but not beaten.

April came and I do not know why, but I sent a birthday card to Lynn, John's estranged ex-wife. I suppose I wanted to reach out to her because I heard how my born-into family had been treating her following John's death. She and John had celebrated more than forty-five years together, including their marriage. John never explained the reason why they divorced, but he did say she was a cheater. I did find out Lynn called my mom and Leslie at least thirty times leading up to his suicide. Lynn's story was that she had begged them to help John because she could not do anything since they were no longer married. After John died, Lynn retired to Florida. I needed more information on everything. Three phone calls later, she asked me to come for a visit. Lynn paid for the airline ticket, and all I had to do was pay for parking at the airport. I thought it was a great idea, so I accepted.

In my mind, I had thoughts of moving to another place. However, that move could not even be contemplated until after Adaline graduated high school. I drove to Toledo, Ohio, where I parked my car and took a flight out. The trip down was beautiful, and there were no incidences. Lynn and I did so much catching up. She was bitter with my born-into family. I told her I no longer was, thanks to much therapy and soul searching. She was impressed and wanted to learn my techniques on coping. I gladly shared my thoughts with Lynn because I felt it was my deeper calling. Over the next week, we planned for me to move down to Florida for the summer.

I came home to Michigan, cancelled my doctor appointments, telling them I was leaving for a couple of months. Pete and I still spoke. He and I decided to have a huge garage sale in his yard. I got rid of many things I was holding on to from childhood. I knew I could let these things go because I no longer cared about my born-into family. I say that with an open heart; I let nothing detour me from my entitlement of happiness. That comment obviously does include Pete. He no longer had the ability to get under my skin. I have, over the years, learned to let it go. I give all my troubles and worries to God, and He really does sustain me. I have forgiven everyone for whatever part they played during my upbringing. I did that for my own inner peace, and guess what? It worked. I was now free and whole.

I drove my vehicle to Florida, throwing Whitney, Elizabeth, and Yousif into tailspins. Whitney cried, Elizabeth wished me well with sadness in her voice, and Yousif was beside himself. He was puzzled to why I was doing it. I explained to him, as I did to Whitney and Elizabeth, I had to get to the bottom of some issues. I was also going to also be doing some small home repairs for Lynn's dad. When I got to Florida, Lynn informed me of the six hundred dollars a month rent fee. I surmised she was bitter with me for having a part of John's money. Lynn did, after all, expect that to be hers.

After pulling myself off the floor, laughing in disbelief, I simply agreed. No, I was not being a pushover. There were amenities.

I was on a selfish mission; one I had every intention of carrying out. I was going to get some much-anticipated information—puzzle pieces, if you will—into John's death. I could care less about the money. Besides, the house was gorgeous and there was a built-in swimming pool. I had planned on enjoying my visit to the fullest, especially if I was paying for it. I was in Florida for clues and facts. I began my investigation as soon as I arrived.

Lynn, in my observation, had not changed at all since my brother died. She did not appear to be sad or remorseful in any way. If anything, she was resentful, and it showed through both her facial expressions and body language. She acted similarly to an immature young teenager. The first evening I was there, she showed me photo albums and John's suicide note. I had only heard the note read by Henry in the sheriff's office in North Carolina. After listening to Lynn read it aloud, I cried for John. I cried for the demons he faced at the end of his life. He was said to have been "paranoid" toward some friends, saying they were using him. They were, in fact, as it was discovered, stealing money and personal items from my brother. That, he was right on about. John was clearly not in a lucid state of mind though. There was, at that time, nothing he could have done differently to prevent their abuse of his mind and pocketbook.

Lynn and I went through numerous photo albums as well. They had a lot of different men in them. She began to brag to me how they were all her lovers since the divorce. Lynn unknowingly assisted me in putting more puzzle pieces together. She also confirmed my suspicions that she had, in fact, been cheating on John during their separation, not only after the divorce. Something John confided in me that he himself felt was going on. She had, by showing me these pictures and giving explanations to whom they were, opened the door for me to lay out some questions that needed answering. I did just that.

I found out those men all had careers that were considered lay work and she was a doctor. She enjoyed talking down about those whom she believed were beneath her. I witnessed it and felt it firsthand, and now she was spewing out her truths. I found that John was, in fact, correct in his assumptions about Lynn's infidelities. She was a bigger shark then imagined, having had multiple affairs on my brother. Here it was, all the proof I needed, sitting at my knees. I felt, deep in my heart, she perpetrated much of the paranoia John had experienced. Lynn did things to make him suspicious and that led to paranoia as she denied it. She admitted to me she had him in and out of court, over what I considered, childish things. All of my information was gathered from the words that sang from Lynn's lips. *Shameful! Pathetic! Criminal!* I felt.

I, at the same time, began splitting household chores with Lynn. I had a lot to do outside and some things inside. I did, quite frequently, feel like hired help, but here I was, giving my *sister* six hundred dollars a month. *No way,* I thought. I was in constant contact with Whitney and Yousif during that time. Whitney was actually listening to the clues I had gathered and was giving me advice.

Yousif did not like the way Lynn was treating me, and neither did I. It was reminiscent of being a child again and doing chores. I was exhausted after working. No more! I just could not do it any longer. Within one week, Yousif was at the airport in Florida, waiting for me to pick him up. He was an amazing friend who did not want to see me get hurt. We got back to Lynn's, and I went into the kitchen to make dinner. I do not know what was said between Lynn and Yousif, but he did not think much of her. He said, "I don't care if she's a doctor; she's stupid." I should mention, Yousif is a very intelligent man and great judge of character. He stayed a week, during which time he convinced me to pack up and leave right away. I had about three weeks left, which worked out, where rent was concerned. Yousif said, "Forget the money, Barb, your mind is more important." So I did. Sometimes, money is paper and your mind is your being. I chose my being.

I waited until the week after Yousif left to pack up my belongings and loaded them into my van. If I had told Lynn earlier, she would have had me leave. She was very petty and childlike when it came to situations like that. I was again a new Barb. Therapy strengthened me. I was not going to let anyone treat me badly, or put me on the hot burner. Lynn owed me money back from the rent that I pre-paid her. She gave me three quarters of it back. The difference was the plane ticket. I suppose she thought I was staying. I was done, and she was definitely finished having me as a sister. Lynn proved to me she treated John like a mat, wiping her feet on his heart and mind, picking away at his psyche. She was under the impression I was another mat. No way was I going to have that happen.

While in my last days of being in Florida, I took full advantage of the beach and weather. I sat on the sand, turning tan before returning home. I had money saved, which had never happened before. I prayed my luck would change, and it did. As I drove through the city the morning before I left, I received a phone call from an apartment complex. They were located in Clinton Township with a two-bedroom opening. What perfect timing. Once again, God was in the driver's seat of my life, and I was so elated. I packed up, leaving Florida, never to look back. I was happy having received many pieces to my brother John's life. I felt relieved and grounded.

I moved into my apartment within three months of coming back. During the time of wait, I stayed with Whitney, and we bonded even deeper. I loved her more than I ever did. She understood me like no other. When you share a friendship with someone for as long of a span as we have had, you really get to know their heart. We are sisters in every sense of the word. I feel God had blessed me in a huge way by bringing Whitney into my life. I reflected on my Florida trip often while staying with Whitney. How quick I was, I thought, to let all of my friend's hands go, not to mention my belongings to strangers at a garage sale. However, there was the bigger picture, and that was the piece of information I took away from the short journey I was on. Ultimately, I did it for John's legacy.

Melonie and Adaline were very happy when I returned from Florida, especially with the way Auntie Lynn was acting. Adaline had just wished she had been able to go to Florida. She did, however, understand my need to leave. I also told Melonie and Adaline I was going temporarily, and I was coming back. I kept my promise to them both, and that was an amazing feeling. They were closer to me as it appeared. Spending some nights together now, I was totally in my element. That was my happy zone, my self-comforting, fabulously therapeutic place.

After seven years with the same nonprofit therapy office, I graduated from their program. I received the best treatment I could have gotten, from an organization that truly cared about their client's recovery. I was told, if there was such a thing as remission from bipolar 1, I was in it. I was finally done with therapy, and I began to see an independent psychiatrist for periodical medication reviews. Becoming the woman, I have metamorphosed into is something I am thoroughly proud of. It was, at times, unbearably difficult. However, with perseverance and determination, anyone in any circumstance can change their life. It is all in how you look at your surroundings. I always walk in gratitude. Those very things that are made to break you are the very things that, in the end, will show your strengths.

I learned, quite quickly, not only was Pete perturbed that I had an apartment; he was still talking his smack about me. Melonie and Adaline, I knew, were smart young girls. They felt the love of my heart and knew I loved them. What Pete did now, had absolutely no effect on me. I had no reason at that point in my life to create any type of animosity between him and myself. That certainly would have been foolish. I loved my daughters and had them back in my space, if only for a bit of time. Melonie was nineteen and living with her boyfriend, and Adaline, now seventeen, was in eleventh grade. They proved to have their own wonderful lives and I was only privy to a small part of it. It was amazing to me how, after all I had done to keep them safe, it was ultimately Pete they ran to. He was their friend. I was still parenting, but from a distance.

I had, on occasion, asked Melonie and Adaline if they were interested in visiting my mom. Their response had always been a resounding no. Adaline's reply was "Why should I?" I cannot say I blame her. My mom did nothing but scar my girls in such a way they lost part of their childhood and innocence. Grandma B thinks money will bring them to her and she is so incorrect. My children did not deserve the treatment they received. I teach them to pass on their knowledge. Forgiveness is for the forgiver, not the one you are forgiving. Repeat that and let it sink into your mind. Melonie is old enough today, that if she wanted to, she could drive to see my mom. She could even go so far as to do it without my knowledge. That actually would be fine with me. We are all entitled to figure things out and in our own ways and within our own timing.

Always rejoice in the Lord. Again, I will say, rejoice! Let your reasonableness become known to all men. The Lord is near. Do not be anxious over anything, but in everything by prayer and supplication along with thanksgiving, let your petitions be made known to God; and the peace of God that surpasses all understanding will guard your hearts and your mental powers by means of Jesus Christ.
—Philippians 4:4–7

CHAPTER 31

I was at an appointment with my new psychiatrist, and I was nudged by God. He instructed me to get up and look at the bulletin board. I actually said no to God. He said so clearly to me, *"Get up and look at the board!"* I was listening the second time. I walked over and saw a pamphlet with colorful graphics. I took it down and began to read it. There was a particular job being advertised, and at that point in time, I had only heard of the title. I had contemplated having that particular job as a new career, and now here it was in print, no longer a dream. The position, which was available was for a Peer-to-Peer Support Specialist. I returned to my seat, and there it was again, the nudge to get up; I had apparently forgotten something. There was also a newsletter. I took it.

I was done with my session and scheduling my next appointment; I thumbed through the newsletter. I came across an organization that I had just done a 5K walk for in September of the previous year. I walked in the event on behalf of John and myself. I found this particular nonprofit resource, National Alliance on Mental Illness (NAMI), which was in every major city, and their specialty was spreading mental health awareness. There was a particular mental health support group they were offering. I thought it was an opportune time for getting back involved with my peers to receive some additional support. The information relayed to me after that one phone call catapulted me into something greater than I could have imagined. My destiny was on the verge of becoming wholly transformed.

I was told the group I contacted was support for the families and loved ones who dealt with the illness firsthand. The group I was in search of had not formed as of that time. I was informed the local chapter in my county was looking for a mental health facilitator. I went to a meeting where I met two wonderful women and a room full of family members. They expressed the urgency for a group where their loved ones could go. It was a gathering that I myself was in search of. Now we were discussing it in detail, and I was extremely interested in getting the facilitator position. It was, in fact, an opportunity for me to slide right in, for an opportunity I had literally only dreamed of.

After listening to those family members speak, I was moved many times to tears. I sat and took notes on possible solutions to problems their mentally ill loved ones faced daily in their lives. I quickly realized those people who had the illness were truly in a state of confusion over the very afflictions I had felt. They had other diagnoses also, which were within my realm of knowledge. I had wanted to help for a long time, and now I was introduced to what could become a great volunteer position. Little did I know, I was being interviewed during the family meeting. Elation! I quickly spoke with one of the women from the group the following morning, and she confirmed it. I was asked to go to training within the month.

I became certified, beginning my journey as the first facilitator for the program offered in our county. Returning from class was a natural high. I researched several locations where it would be conducive for us, as a whole, to gather together. Within one month of being trained, our group was up and running. I think God does, in fact, help individuals who help themselves. I have worked diligently to improve my life, and most importantly, to make better choices. The volunteer position proved to be a fabulous stepping stone for my ongoing plans to be a life coach. While my immediate goal was to become a Peer-to-Peer Support Specialist, I found the volunteer position covered a multitude of jobs. I enjoyed this responsibility immensely.

One morning, I received a call from an old friend of mine. Lana, whom I was close to from the scouting days with my daughters, inquired if I would be interested to fill in for her at work while she went on vacation. It was a two-week engagement, and I jumped on my favorable time for abundance. I figured it was an excellent chance to get back into working.

The particular position involved being a drug lab technician. Ultimately, the people I tested were, in fact, me years earlier. I was able to empathize with them, yet give them advice they could truly benefit from. I enjoyed working the assignment, no matter how short a time, believing I made a difference in someone's life. Once Lana returned, I began looking steadily for jobs in my given fields of expertise. I talked with the gentleman in charge of the organization with whom I volunteered for, and he gave me the schedule for additional training. I had decided to pursue a career in helping others with issues that I myself overcame. Unfortunately, I would have to wait seven months for the upcoming class, so I used the time to research public speaking and presentations.

I was a regular staple at the local library, taking book after book out, reading them all. It became a passion of mine, gathering as much information as possible before the actual training. The subject matter which I read encompassed informative outreach tools for mental health recovery. My main objective, after much research, was to go into local police and sheriff' stations, juvenile halls, and the corporate communities. I found myself planning extensively to introduce myself as to what the many faces of mental illness may look like. The objective was for me to educate others regarding intimidation and stigma against those having mental issues. I want to bring information to those very people who are ill, giving them the many tools they need, to make heartfelt and informed decisions. People fear what they do not know. This subject is a substantial one too. I stopped for a moment, taking it all in. I was living the dream I put into my head at an early age, to be an educator on mental health—here I was!

Melonie was working herself into making quite a little nest egg. I barely saw her but missed her daily. Adaline and I chatted quite frequently; and she and I had fun, with sleepovers at my place, in months prior. I love my daughters unconditionally, and I am confident they will come to see that as they mature. I believe we three appreciate each other for our individual and special talents. Adaline was in her senior year, involving herself in sewing, making cosplay, and filling out college applications. Preparing for college was another adventure Adaline took on. Both of my daughters grew to be very intelligent and wise. I love that they have common sense in an age when young adults lack that. My girls are my joy and hope for future years to come. I have also learned, a daughter, no matter how independent, will come back to her mom when she is ready. I will *not* tell you that the negative effects from Pete's abusive mouth have not affected my daughter's opinion of me. After all, they have been hearing that ruckus for fourteen years. Consciously, I have tried and to keep my opinions of Pete to myself. However, I admit to being human. Pete has knowingly continued his negative talk about me, even after being divorced for several years. Be it old neighbors, friends, or my daughters, he was weighed down by his cesspool way of thinking. Pete's insecurities plague him still. We, as individuals, must consistently strive to remain true to ourselves at all costs. I am a mom first and foremost. Pete can never take that away from me. I bore those girls, and they are every bit of him as they are me. I firmly believe, in growing older, my daughters will see the whole picture for themselves.

Even though I tell them verbally how beautiful, funny, and talented they are, I encourage my daughters. Encouragement is something I never received from my born-into family. I will continue that until the day I am no longer here. That is my God-given job, and my honor, to pass down to them all I have learned. They are somewhat grown now, and as a mom, I delight in embracing their individual uniqueness. I love the fact they both continue developing independence, and in doing so, they will fully blossom into the wonderful women God intended them to be.

Whitney and I communicated multiple times a week. We consider ourselves to be each other's earth angels and best friends forever. God wrote that in his book of life, no doubt. Being that social media is so widely used today, we both have reconnected with many friends from our high school days. Our school friends have get-togethers multiple times a year; many of us keep in touch outside of that too. I see Brian and Martin from home economics class often. They grew up to be funny adults. Elizabeth and I see each other monthly. She has remained my longest relationship, spanning over forty-two years. It is a wonderful feeling, to be able to pick and choose your own family, the extraordinary people who surround you through good times and hard lessons. I have learned, those whom you hold closely to in memories are the one with whom you never really lost a connection with, in the here and now. I have also learned it is the quality, not quantity, when choosing forever friends. Yousif remains my closest male friend to this day. His contagious attitude is a delight. It is important to be around others who are more knowledgeable in different areas. That way, you are continuously learning, growing, and maturing.

I became happily comfortable with my living arrangements and actually loved my personal space. I share it with my two cats, Lynear and Fandango. They both constantly prove to be the best therapy cats a girl could love. I have experienced, over the course of my life, the animals who I took in, crossed my path with their own purpose…one to take to heart. They gave unconditional love to me when no one else did. I am forever grateful to every one of them. There was never a term such as "therapy animals" when I was growing up; however, that is what they all provided to me. I would never imagine that having a pet lick my tears away, compassionate looks into my eyes, and those gentle nudges with their heads could fulfill me the way in which it did. All the animals I have loved, provided me unconditional acceptance, comradery, and affection—three things I never received from my born-into family.

Through the course of living, I have gathered insight. Without my *faith, personal perseverance and resilience*, and the *love* for my children, I would have most certainly given up, taking my own life. God showed me I was living for a reason, and that is the message. I believe each and every person on earth is here with a divine purpose. You can be an excellent example, or you can be a dreadful warning. I choose to be an inspiration! I want my legacy to be a good and healthy one. I do not want the bad choices from my past determining my future or my memory when I have died from natural causes. I have too much to do in showing that people do change, and go on to bigger and better things. From heartache to happiness, the road *less* travelled *is* the road to take. You do not want to be like everyone else. Cookie-cutter people are boring. Be unique, good-hearted, and learn how to engage in speaking with others. That is where you will learn. Never be hard on yourself for others will do enough of that, and when they do, buffer it. You do not need negativity surrounding you, bring in the positive energy. You will feel like a million dollars for having done so.

I recently was called to work by the nonprofit company I was a fill-in lab technician for. The director decided, with my unbiased personality, past background and mental health experience, I was the perfect fit for his opening. I was trained and began my new career as a Presenter, teaching personal development and addiction prevention. My areas of instruction included high schools and juvenile justice centers. I believe God has seen me through, full circle. Think about this for a moment...I dreamt of being a public speaker, helping others who are now or will go through what I have endured. In both of my positions in working and volunteering, I have satisfied my deepest desires.

I successfully continued to run the mental health group in my county, reaching out to those who need attention, advice, and a listening ear. My co-facilitator and I have helped several, some have been suicidal. Our goal is in changing our group's perspective of not only themselves, but of their circumstances. Unlearn what is not truthful or unhelpful. We encourage, guide, and assist in any way we are able. What a rewarding job. I am exactly where God intended me to be, and I am helping others due to the past experiences I have endured. If I had not been diagnosed with a mental illness, I would not have saved a life. I was able to help to intervene *because* of my illnesses and experiences. Wow! That is amazing. In the spring of 2017, I continued my education with NAMI, taking an additional class for my volunteering. In Our Own Voice allows me the ability to go into the private sectors, police departments, jails, and schools.

The aspirations I have for my life have just begun, in a sense. I have had to live through the hellacious times to reap these wonderful rewards. The ultimate goal now is to give back to others all that I have learned over the years, with respect to drugs, alcohol, and mental illness. We are all here with a divine purpose. Remember that!

Always take to heart the things that matter most. *Faith* in God, *love* for life, *goodwill* toward others and *comradery* among your chosen family of friends. Materialist things come and go, true friends and knowledge stay forever. Anything that God allows to come our way is always with a purpose. He uses even the greatest errors and deepest pains to mold us into being better people. You must remember, you too have to be proactive in your future. It does not matter if you are twenty years old or seventy years old. There is always time to improve one's self. Even if we are surrounded with disappointments and heartache all our lives, there is a greater purpose. Stay strong and firm; you have the power to overcome your demons. I am living proof.

RESOURCES

National Alliance on Mental Illness (NAMI): A grassroots, nonprofit organization having a plethora of information on mental illness, for those with the illness and the family members who support them. USA wide. *nami.org*

Therapy Animals: An animal aiding in helping an individual with many illnesses. Usually a domestic animal. The premise is that in giving love to the animal, the owner receives unconditional love back.

Dailystrength.org: A website with an array of help groups geared toward specific illnesses. Find your topic and sign on.

National Institute of Mental Health (NIMH): Government agency with information on mental illness.

Mental Health.gov: Resources for all health issues affecting your mental mind.

American Foundation For Suicide Prevention: 1-800-273-TALK (8255) or the Crisis Text Line by texting TALK to 741741. *afsp.org*

Easter Seals: An all-encompassing organization who aids in the recovery and resources for those who have disabilities, so that they may live full and healthy lives!

There are obviously more resources available. These are mine. Please feel free to check the internet out to find additional websites which will help you overcome your ailment. *Awareness and proactivity are the keys to success.*

ABOUT THE AUTHOR

As an individual, B. A. Marks is not only determined to make a difference in this world; she has proven to be relevant to society. Even though her family did not embrace her, optimism was not difficult for Barb to achieve, for it was breathed into her by God Himself. Educating and teaching our youth and mental health advocacy are passions for Barb. Every young adult she comes in contact with feels her empathy and nonjudgmental love. Educating others on mental illness acceptance and terminating the stigma associated with those illnesses will be a cause that Barb will indefinitely advocate for. Barb's goal is to touch as many hearts as possible, letting them know, that they too are relevant to society!